©2021

Photography Contributions by:
Exceed Nutrition
Lisa Severn @rhubarbstreet
Paula Owen @paulaowenphotography

The Balanced Four Cookbook

Simple, healthy recipe for your busy life.

Jessi McLennan NNCP

Dedication

For my family.

Thank you for the never ending support, the lessons, the silliness and *ALL* the giggles.

Contents

Introduction 7

Breakfast 14

Salads 28

Soup, Plant Based, Fish 46

Chicken & Turkey 66

Pasta & Stir Fry 86

Beef & Pork 102

Snacks & Treats 114

Index 124

Introduction

Thank you for choosing The Balanced Four Cookbook. It means so much to me knowing I get to share in a little part of your day.

This book is all about helping you create healthy, delicious meals that are quick and easy, save you time and stress in the kitchen and help you live your healthiest life.

As a registered nutrition coach and practitioner, busy mama of 2 and food lover, it's really important to me to create recipes that are not only healthy and balanced but can be on the table in less than 30 minutes.

Each recipe follows my simple formula for creating a balanced meal, by combining protein, color, slow carbs and healthy fat. You'll find ideas (in the notes section) on how to adapt a recipe to meet specific needs, create a vegetarian version or change up certain ingredients to appease little taste buds.

All recipes start with whole, unprocessed foods. This truly is one of the only diet 'rules' that I follow - choosing food and ingredients as close to their natural state as possible. However, you'll find that I still use time saving ingredients like pre-made pasta sauce or curry paste, canned tomatoes or frozen fruits and vegetables. Because, I believe life is not about being perfect, it's about doing the best you can in the time you have.

On the next few pages you'll find some helpful resources to get yourself set up for success in the kitchen, along with some time saving tips to help you get organized with meal planning and prep.

Healthy eating doesn't need to be complicated, cost a fortune or require hours in the kitchen. I hope the recipes and meal planning tips in this book help you to reduce the meal time hustle so you can focus on living your best life.

From my kitchen to yours. Enjoy.

The 4 Key Components

Creating a balanced diet starts with 4 key components; protein, color, slow carbs and health fat. Each group has a different role to play and is essential for good health. All recipes in The Balanced Four Cookbook combine these components to create balanced meals.

1 Protein

- stimulates muscle growth and repair
- stabilizes blood sugar level
- helps to control appetite
- supports immune function

Good sources: fish, meat, poultry, tofu, eggs, beans, nuts and seeds

2 Color

- provides essential vitamins & minerals
- contains an excellent source of fiber
- provides disease fighting antioxidants and phytochemicals

Good sources: colorful fruits & vegetables

3 Slow Carbs

- help stabilize blood sugar levels
- promote satiety (feeling full)
- provide an excellent source of fiber which can improve digestion and gut health

Good sources: beans, lentils, whole grains, most fruits & vegetables

4 Healthy Fat

- essential for healthy brain function and mood regulation
- plays a role in hormone production
- can reduce inflammation
- encourages the absorption of some vitamins and mineral

Good sources: nuts, seeds, avocado, eggs, olive oil, salmon and other fatty fish

Creating a Balanced Meal

Most recipes in The Balanced Four Cookbook follow a simple formula that combines the 4 key components. You can use this formula to create your own healthy meals or balance out some of your favorites. Now, of course all meals are going to look slightly different and you may need to adjust this formula to meet your specific needs, but if you keep the following image in mind, you're well on your way to creating a balanced meal.

Color
Fill half the plate with colorful vegetables.

Protein
A quarter of the plate is reserved for protein rich food.

Healthy Fat
Add healthy fat from a variety of different sources.

Slow Carbs
Slow carbs take up the remaining quarter of the plate.

Pantry Essentials

A well stocked pantry makes it easier to put together quick & healthy meals and snacks. The ingredients below are some of the key items that I always have in *my* pantry and you'll find them used in the recipes throughout the cookbook.

HERBS & SPICES

- Basil
- Chili flakes
- Chili powder
- Cinnamon
- Cumin
- Curry powder
- Garlic powder
- Italian seasoning
- Onion powder
- Oregano
- Paprika
- Rosemary
- Salt & Pepper
- Taco seasoning (p. 81)
- Turmeric

CONDIMENTS (FRIDGE), OILS, NUTS & SEEDS

- Balsamic vinegar
- Broth concentrate (beef, chicken & vegetable)
- Hot sauce
- Mustard (yellow & Dijon)
- Pesto
- Salsa
- Soy Sauce/Tamari sauce
- Sriracha Sauce
- Avocado oil (or other cooking oil)
- Avocado oil spray (or other cooking spray)
- Butter
- Coconut oil
- Extra virgin olive oil
- Sesame oil
- Almonds
- Chia seeds
- Ground flax seed
- Hemp seeds
- Peanuts
- Pecans
- Pumpkin seeds
- Sunflower seeds
- Walnuts

PANTRY ESSENTIALS & DRY GOODS

- Canned beans (chickpeas, black beans etc.)
- Coconut milk
- Corn flour/starch
- Curry paste
- Diced tomatoes
- Pasta noodles
- Pasta Sauce
- Passata (tomato puree)
- Quinoa
- Quick oats
- Refried beans
- Rice (jasmine, basmati, brown)
- Rice noodles
- Rice paper
- Rolled oats
- Taco or Tostada shells
- Tomato paste
- Whole grain bread or wraps

To cut down on the time you spend in the kitchen, there's a couple of key kitchen tools that will make your life so much easier! The basic's are your *foundation*, these are the things that will simplify your day to day meal prep.

THE BASICS

- 4-5 different sized pots & pans
- 2-3 different sized skillets/fry pans
- 12 hole muffin tin
- Assortment of mixing bowls
- Baking trays (cookie sheets)
- Blender
- Box grater
- Casserole dishes (varying sizes)
- Chef's knife & knife sharpener
- Checkered/wire cooling racks
- Chopping boards (at least 1 wooden & 1 plastic)
- Fine mesh sieve/strainer/colander
- Food processor
- Freezer safe zip lock bags
- Garlic press
- Glass, snap lid containers
- Ice cube trays
- Immersion blender
- Instant pot/pressure cooker
- Measuring cups, jugs and spoons
- Reusable storage containers
- Slow cooker/Crockpot
- Steamer insert for saucepan

6-Step Meal Prep

Meal planning and prep helps you stay organized during the week and stay on track with healthy, balanced eating.

Completing even just 1-2 tasks will help to simplify the meal time hustle.

1. CREATE YOUR MEAL PLAN

- ◯ Place it where you can see it
- ◯ Keep your plan for future use
- ◯ Plan easy meals for busy days
- ◯ Set aside 1 day for M.Y.O.D* night or to use up leftovers in the fridge

2. COOK OR PREP CARBS

- ◯ Cook rice or quinoa
- ◯ Cook potatoes
- ◯ Cook edamame (for snacks or Buddha bowl) or rinse beans

3. PREP PROTEIN

- ◯ Grill or bake chicken for lunches
- ◯ Boil eggs
- ◯ Marinade or prep meat for weeknight meals

4. PREP VEGETABLES

- ◯ Wash & dry veggies if needed
- ◯ Chop veggies for weeknight meals
- ◯ Chop veggies for snacks

5. PREP SNACKS & FRUIT

- ◯ Wash & dry fruit if needed
- ◯ Chop fruit for snacks
- ◯ Make chia pudding
- ◯ Make a batch of energy balls
- ◯ Portion out nuts or trail mix
- ◯ Make snack packs by combining cut up veggies & 1/4 cup of hummus

6. PREP BREKAFAST

- ◯ Overnight oats (pg. 15)
- ◯ Egg muffins (pg.22)
- ◯ Breakfast burritos (pg. 21)
- ◯ Chia pudding (pg. 25)

*M.Y.O.D = make your own dinner night.
If you have kids, let them choose (and make) their own dinner (with ingredients your already have in the house).

10 Minute Tasks

Meal prepping doesn't have to mean doing ALL of your meal prep ALL at once. If you have a busy schedule or your weekends are full of activities, family commitments or kids sports, you may find it more helpful (and more do-able) to split your meal prep activities into smaller tasks.

When you find you have a spare 10 minutes - maybe you're waiting for dinner to finish cooking or you've got 10 minutes in the morning before heading to work or dropping the kids off to school - use this list and complete 1-2 simple tasks. All these small steps add up to big wins throughout the week. Each task takes between 5-10 minutes.

- Wash and dry fruit and vegetables
- Chop vegetables for snacks
- Chop fruit for snacks
- Make chia pudding (pg. 25,115)
- Make overnight oats (pg. 15)
- Boil eggs for snacks
- Chop vegetables for dinner
- Cook rice or quinoa for lunches
- Steam Edamame
- Check your freezer and make a list of any meals that you can add to your weekly meal plan*
- Scramble eggs for breakfast burritos (pg.21)

*Freezer meals are a life saver for busy nights. We host freezer-prep workshops in the Balanced Four membership. Find out more by using the QR code on page 127.

Breakfast

Apple & Cinnamon Oatmeal

Overnight Oats

Granola

Muesli

Warm Barley Breakfast

Breakfast Smoothie

Avocado French Toast with Egg

Breakfast Burritos

Egg Muffins

Eggs with Sweet Potato Toast

Fried Egg Breakfast Salad

Vanilla Banana Chia Pudding

Apple and Cinnamon Oatmeal

2 SERVINGS 10 MINUTES

INGREDIENTS

2/3 cup Oats
1 Apple (diced)
1 tsp Cinnamon
1 tsp Vanilla Extract
2 cups Water
1/4 cup Pecans (chopped)

NUTRITION

AMOUNT PER SERVING

Calories	242	**Fiber**	7g
Fat	11g	**Sugar**	11g
Carbs	34g	**Protein**	5g

DIRECTIONS

01 Combine all ingredients (apart from pecans) in a medium sized cooking pot and mix well.

02 Bring to a boil, reduce heat and simmer for 10-15 mins, stirring occasionally. Add additional water if required.

03 Serve topped with pecans, a small drizzle of honey and a splash of milk if desired.

NOTES

TIME SAVER
Place ingredients in a large microwave safe bowl and microwave for 2 minutes, stir and cook for an additional 2 minutes.

PROTEIN BOOST
Add 1 scoop (1/4 cup) vanilla protein powder - you may need to add additional liquid.

MAKE IT CREAMY
Combine 1 cup of water with 1 cup of milk (of choice) for a creamier texture.

NO PECANS
Use chopped almonds, walnuts or seeds instead.

Overnight Oats

3 SERVINGS 5 MINUTES

INGREDIENTS

1 cup Rolled Oats
1/2 cup Milk (of choice)
1/2 cup Apple Juice
1 cup Frozen Berries
1 cup Plain Yogurt
1/4 cup Walnuts Or Almond (chopped)
2 tbsps Chia Seeds Or Ground Flax
1/2 tsp Cinnamon
1 tsp Vanilla Extract

NUTRITION

AMOUNT PER SERVING

Calories	318	Fiber	7g
Fat	11g	Sugar	18g
Carbs	42g	**Protein**	13g

DIRECTIONS

01 Combine all ingredients in a large container or divide into smaller single serve containers. Leave to soak overnight in the refrigerator.

NOTES

MILK
Use any type of milk you like - almond, coconut, cashew, dairy etc.

VARIATIONS
Start with a base of 1:1:1 (equal parts of oats, yogurt and liquid – milk or juice). Create different flavors by using a different juice base, use a flavored yogurt, try diced mango, kiwi fruit or grated apple instead of berries.

REDUCE SUGAR
Leave out the juice and make up the difference by adding extra milk.

STORGAE
Keep in the fridge for 3 days. You may need to add a little extra liquid before serving.

TOO THICK?
Add additional milk or juice.

INCREASE PROTEIN
Use Greek yogurt or add 2 tbsp. protein powder to the mix, add an additional 1/4 cup of milk or juice.

Granola

16 SERVINGS 50 MINUTES

INGREDIENTS

4 cups Rolled Oats
4 ozs Apple Juice (1/2 cup)
2 tbsps Maple Syrup
2 tbsps Coconut Oil
1 tsp Vanilla Extract
1/4 cup Pumpkin Seeds
1/4 cup Sunflower Seeds
1/2 cup Pecans (chopped)
1/2 cup Dried Cranberries
1 tsp Cinnamon
1/4 cup Hemp Seeds
1/4 cup Unsweetened Shredded Coconut

NUTRITION

AMOUNT PER SERVING

Calories	181	Fiber	3g
Fat	9g	Sugar	6g
Carbs	23g	Protein	4g

DIRECTIONS

01 Preheat oven to 350F. Line a large baking sheet with baking paper.

02 In a large bowl combine oats, cinnamon, apple juice, maple syrup vanilla and coconut oil. Mix well making sure all ingredients are well combined. Spread the granola onto a large baking sheet.

03 Bake for 15 minutes, remove from oven, add pecans (or other nuts) and stir. Replace, and bake for another 15-20 minutes, stirring an additional 1-2 times to ensure even cooking.

04 Remove from oven and stir through coconut, seeds and dried fruit. Allow to completely cool before storing in an airtight container.

NOTES

NUTS & SEEDS
Substitute pecans with almonds, walnuts, pistachio or macadamia nuts.

BOOST PROTEIN
Add 1 scoop vanilla protein powder the oats before adding the apple juice. Increase apple juice by 1/4 cup.

DRIED FRUIT
Swap dried cranberries for any other dried fruit, including apricots, apple, papaya etc.

SERVING SIZE
1 serving = 1/3 cup

Muesli

16 SERVINGS 10 MINUTES

INGREDIENTS

4 cups Oats (rolled)
1/4 cup Unsweetened Shredded Coconut
1/4 cup Sliced Almonds
1/4 cup Flax Seed
1/4 cup Dried Apricots (diced)
1/4 cup Raisins
1/4 cup Pumpkin Seeds
1/4 cup Sunflower Seeds

NUTRITION

AMOUNT PER SERVING

Calories	141	Fiber	4g
Fat	6g	Sugar	3g
Carbs	19g	**Protein**	5g

DIRECTIONS

01 Combine all ingredients in a large bowl.

02 Transfer to a large, airtight container. Enjoy!

NOTES

STORAGE Keep in an airtight container for up to 2 months.

SERVE WITH Yogurt, fresh fruit or berries and a sprinkle of hemp seeds.

VARIATIONS Use any combination of dried fruit, nuts and seeds that you like.

Warm Barley Breakfast

8 SERVINGS 40 MINUTES

INGREDIENTS

1 cup Pearl Barley
2 cups Apple Juice
2 cups Milk (of choice)
2 tsps Vanilla Extract
1 cup Frozen Mango (diced)
2 cups Plain Greek Yogurt
2 cups Blueberries
1 tsp Lemon Zest (the zest of 1 lemon)
1 tsp Cinnamon

NUTRITION

AMOUNT PER SERVING

Calories	208	Fiber	6g
Fat	2g	Sugar	15g
Carbs	39g	Protein	9g

DIRECTIONS

01 In a large cooking pot, add pearl barley, apple juice, milk of choice, vanilla extract and cinnamon, bring to a boil. Reduce heat, cover and simmer for 30-40 minutes.

02 Stir occasionally to make sure the barley doesn't stick to the bottom.

03 Once barley is cooked (when most the liquid has been absorbed and the barley is soft), stir through diced mango. Take off heat, replace lid and let sit for 5 minutes.

04 Garnish with lemon zest and serve with yogurt and berries.

NOTES

CREATE DIFFERENT FLAVOURS
Use different flavored juice. Substitute the mango for diced apple, dried figs, dried apricots or any other fruit you like.

REDUCE THE CARBS
Use 1 cup of juice instead of 2 and add 1 extra cup of milk.

MILK
Use any milk of your choice including cashew, oat, almond, coconut, dairy, hemp etc.

STORAGE
Keep covered in the fridge for up to 5 days. You may need to add a little extra milk as the barley will continue to absorb liquid while in the fridge.

Breakfast Smoothie

1 SERVING 5 MINUTES

INGREDIENTS

1/4 cup Vanilla Protein Powder (1scoop)
1/2 Frozen Banana
1/2 cup Frozen Berries
1 tbsp Ground Flax Seed
1 1/2 cups Water or milk of choice

NUTRITION

AMOUNT PER SERVING

Calories	213	Fiber	6g
Fat	3g	Sugar	15g
Carbs	27g	**Protein**	22g

DIRECTIONS

01 Place all ingredients into a blender and mix until well combined.

NOTES

NO FLAXSEED
Use chia or hemp or add 1 tbsp of almond or peanut butter instead of the seeds.

VARIATIONS
Use any combination of frozen fruit you like. Keep the serving size to 3/4 - 1 cup of fruit.

FOR CHOCOLATE LOVERS
Add 2 tsp cocoa powder or use a chocolate protein powder.

NUTRITION BOOST
Add a handful of baby spinach or kale, a teaspoon of spirulina, maca or your favorite supplement boost.

Avocado French Toast with Egg

1 SERVING 15 MINUTES

INGREDIENTS

2 slices Whole Grain Bread (or gluten free)
1/4 Avocado
Sea Salt & Black Pepper (to taste)
2 Egg
1 tbsp Milk (of choice)

NUTRITION

AMOUNT PER SERVING

Calories	451	Fiber	10g
Fat	21g	Sugar	7g
Carbs	42g	**Protein**	25g

DIRECTIONS

01 Break one egg into a shallow bowl, add milk and lightly whisk.

02 Cut avocado in half, remove the pit and cut into fine slices. Mash and season with a little salt and pepper to taste.

03 Spread avocado on bread and place other piece on top.

04 Gently dip the avocado sandwich into the egg mixture, coating each side. Let any excess egg drip off. Place into a preheated skillet. Cook for 2-3 minutes per side or until golden brown.

05 Cook the second egg to your liking and serve on top of the toasted avocado sandwich.

Breakfast Burritos

4 SERVINGS 20 MINUTES

INGREDIENTS

8 Egg (lightly beaten)
4 Whole Grain Tortilla Wraps
1 Tomato (diced)
2 cups Baby Spinach (shredded)
2 ozs Natural Ham (diced)
2 ozs Cheddar Cheese (grated)
1/2 cup Salsa

NUTRITION

AMOUNT PER SERVING

Calories	454	Fiber	5g
Fat	19g	Sugar	4g
Carbs	41g	**Protein**	25g

DIRECTIONS

01 Add eggs to a large, non-stick skillet and cook over medium heat, moving the egg around the pan until scrambled and fully cooked.

02 Divide egg and remaining ingredients between tortilla wraps and roll them up like a burrito.

03 Serve as is or place rolled up wraps into a large skillet to crisp up the sides.

NOTES

FREEZE BURRITOS AS PART OF YOUR MEAL PREP
If preparing for the freezer, allow burrito to completely cool. Wrap each burrito tightly with cling wrap or wax paper. Place burritos in a freezer bag, gently squeeze out as much air as possible and seal bag. Place in freezer for up to 2 months.

TO RE-HEAT
To reheat breakfast burrito, remove from freezer, remove cling wrap and place in the microwave for 1 ½-2 minutes depending on microwave, or reheat at 350F for 20 minutes.

ADD ADDITIONAL VEGGIES
Use any combination of vegetables you like including, mushrooms, onions, peppers, leftover roasted vegetables etc.

REDUCE CARBS
Swap the tortilla wrap for large Swiss Chard leaves. Remove the stem and place the egg mixture and other ingredients in the middle of the leaf. Roll up just like a burrito.

REDUCE FAT
Use 4 whole eggs and 1 cup of egg white.

Ham, Cheese, Tomato, Breakfast Egg Muffins

4 SERVINGS 35 MINUTES

INGREDIENTS

9 Egg
1 cup Baby Spinach (shredded)
1 Tomato (diced)
1/2 White Onion (diced)
2 ozs Natural Ham (diced or cut into strips)
1/2 tsp Black Pepper
2 ozs Cheddar Cheese (grated)

NUTRITION

AMOUNT PER SERVING

Calories	262	Fiber	1g
Fat	17g	Sugar	2g
Carbs	4g	Protein	20g

DIRECTIONS

01 Preheat oven to 350°F. Lightly grease 12 holes of a muffin pan with oil or use cooking spray.

02 Sauté onion for 3-4 minutes. Add spinach and cook for another 1 minute or until spinach has wilted and is bright green.

03 Divide onion, spinach, tomato, ham and cheese between prepared muffin pan.

04 In a large mixing bowl, lightly beat eggs, add pepper and salt to season.

05 Pour the whisked eggs into the muffin cups, covering the vegetables.

06 Bake for 20-25 minutes or until the egg is cooked through and no longer liquid on top. Remove from oven.

07 Eat straight away or store in the fridge for up to 4 days.

NOTES

SERVING SIZE
1 serving is equal to 3 egg muffins (if you fill 12 cups).

VARIATIONS
Use any combo of veggies and add additional protein if you like.

REDUCE FAT
Use 5 whole eggs and 1/2 cup egg white.

Eggs with Sweet Potato Toast

1 SERVING 10 MINUTES

INGREDIENTS

2 Egg

3 pieces Sweet Potato (cut into 1/2" rounds, approximately 3 oz.)

1/2 Tomato (sliced)

1/2 cup Baby Spinach

1/2 tsp Extra Virgin Olive Oil

1/2 Pear (or other type of fruit)

NUTRITION

AMOUNT PER SERVING

Calories	324	Fiber	7g
Fat	12g	Sugar	9g
Carbs	39g	**Protein**	16g

DIRECTIONS

01 Wash sweet potato (leave skin on), cut three large rounds, approximately 1/2" thick. Place on a large plate with 1 tbsp water. Microwave for 2 minutes. Place in a toaster and cook for 2-3 rounds.

02 Add oil to a small skillet and cook eggs to your liking.

03 Place spinach and tomato on top of sweet potato, arrange eggs on top. Serve with a piece of sliced fruit or berries.

NOTES

WHY MICROWAVE?
This cuts down on the amount of time it takes for the 'toast' to become soft on the inside but crispy on the outside. If you don't have a microwave, toast the sweet potato and extra 2-3 times in the toaster.

SWEET POTATO OR YAM?
Sweet potato = orange flesh. This is one VERY confusing topic as often these terms are used interchangeably. However, in all of my recipes, a sweet potato will always refer to the oranges fleshed root vegetable.

Fried Egg Breakfast Salad

1 SERVING 10 MINUTES

INGREDIENTS

2 Egg
2 cups Baby Spinach
1/2 cup Cherry Tomatoes
1/4 Avocado
1/4 Red Bell Pepper (cut into 2 rings)
1/4 cup Strawberries

NUTRITION

AMOUNT PER SERVING

Calories	256	Fiber	6g
Fat	17g	Sugar	6g
Carbs	12g	**Protein**	15g

DIRECTIONS

01 Slice the red pepper to create 2 rings (deep enough that you can crack the eggs into and they won't spill over the sides). Microwave pepper rings for 1 minute (not essential, but will make them a little softer once done).

02 Heat a non-stick pan and place the peppers in the middle. Crack the eggs into each pepper. Cook eggs to your liking, usually 3-5 minutes. Place a lid over the pan to speed up cooking and to ensure the egg white cooks.

03 Add the spinach, cherry tomatoes and avocado to a plate and top with cooked eggs. Season with salt and pepper if needed. Serve with strawberries.

NOTES

EXTRA VEGGIES
Sauté some mushrooms and onion while the eggs are cooking.

EXTRA FLAVOUR
Drizzle salad with Balsamic reduction or your favorite salad dressing before adding the egg.

Chia Pudding with Banans and Walnuts

2 SERVINGS 10 MINUTES

INGREDIENTS

1/4 cup Chia Seeds

1 cup Unsweetened Oat Milk (or milk of choice)

1 Banana (sliced)

1/2 tsp Cinnamon

2 tbsps Vanilla Protein Powder

2 tsps Maple Syrup

2 tbsps Walnuts (chopped)

NUTRITION

AMOUNT PER SERVING

Calories	322	**Fiber**	10g
Fat	16g	**Sugar**	15g
Carbs	38g	**Protein**	12g

DIRECTIONS

01 In a jar or container, combine chia seeds, oat milk, cinnamon, vanilla protein powder and maple syrup. Use a fork to mix well, secure lid and vigorously shake for 20-30 second. Stir through banana and walnuts. Divide between 2 smaller containers, refrigerate for at least 2 hours or overnight.

NOTES

STORAGE
Store covered in the fridge for up to 4 to 5 days.

NO BANANA
Use berries, sliced peaches or any other fruit.

WRONG CONSISTANCY?
If the chia pudding is too thin, add 1-2 TBSP additional chia, allow to set for an extra 1-2 hours. If the chia pudding is too thick add a small amount of additional liquid.

Salads

Bocconcini, Tomato, Pesto Lunch Bowl

Garden Salad

Lentil, Artichoke & Sundried Tomato Salad

Quinoa Salad

Strawberry, Asparagus & Goats Cheese Salad

Flaked Salmon with Beans & Arugula Salad

Grilled Salmon & Peach Salad

Tuna Stack with Fresh Tomato Salsa

Buffalo Chicken Salad

Broccoli & Bacon Pasta Salad with BBQ Chicken

Goat's Cheese, Prosciutto, Pear & Walnut Salad

Montreal Steak Salad

Warm Roast Vegetable Salad

Bocconcini, Tomato Lunch Bowl

2 SERVINGS 10 MINUTES

INGREDIENTS

2 Large Bocconcini (sliced, approximately 50g, or 1.5 oz)
2 Tomato (small, sliced)
1/2 Avocado
4 ozs Nitrate Free Sliced Turkey Breast
4 cups Mixed Greens
2 tbsps Pesto

DIRECTIONS

01 Arrange all ingredients in a bowl or container and top with pesto.

NOTES

NO TURKEY
Use nitrate-free ham, roast beef, smoked salmon, grilled chicken.

NUTRITION

AMOUNT PER SERVING

Calories	368	Fiber	5g
Fat	24g	Sugar	2g
Carbs	14g	**Protein**	25g

Garden Salad

4 SERVINGS 10 MINUTES

INGREDIENTS

1/4 cup Extra Virgin Olive Oil
2 tbsps Balsamic Vinegar
2 tsps Yellow Mustard
1/2 head Green Lettuce (roughly chopped)
2 Tomato (medium, sliced)
1 Cucumber (sliced)
2 Red Bell Pepper
2 Carrot (grated)
1 tsp Italian Seasoning
1 tsp Garlic (crushed)

NUTRITION

AMOUNT PER SERVING

Calories	176	Fiber	3g
Fat	14g	Sugar	6g
Carbs	12g	**Protein**	2g

DIRECTIONS

01 In a small bowl, whisk together the olive oil, mustard, vinegar, Italian seasoning and garlic.

02 Add remaining ingredients to a large bowl and drizzle the dressing over top. Toss until well coated. Divide onto plates and enjoy!

NOTES

NO BALSAMIC VINEGAR
Use red wine vinegar, apple cider vinegar or white vinegar instead.

NO LETTUCE
Use spinach, kale or mixed greens instead.

MORE TOPPINGS
Add sliced red onion, olives, crumbled feta, grated beets and/or avocado.

ON-THE-GO
Keep dressing in a separate container on the side. Add just before serving.

Artichoke, Lentil & Sundried Tomato Salad

2 SERVINGS 10 MINUTES

INGREDIENTS

1 cup Cooked Lentils (rinsed and drained)
2 tbsps Sun Dried Tomatoes (drained)
1/2 cup Artichoke Hearts (drained)
4 cups Baby Spinach (3-4 handfuls)
1/2 Cucumber (chopped)
2 tbsps Tahini
2 tsps Apple Cider Vinegar
1 tsp Tamari (or soy sauce)
1 tsp Honey

NUTRITION

AMOUNT PER SERVING

Calories	264	Fiber	14g
Fat	13g	Sugar	9g
Carbs	35g	**Protein**	15g

DIRECTIONS

01 Prepare dressing by combining tahini, vinegar, tamari & honey, season with salt and pepper.

02 Place all other ingredients in a large bowl and drizzle with dressing. Serve as a side dish or add a portion of protein for a main meal.

NOTES

MAIN MEAL SALAD

Serve with grilled chicken, fish or shrimp or add additional lentils to boost protein.

Quinoa Salad

4 SERVINGS 20 MINUTES

INGREDIENTS

1 cup Quinoa (rinsed)
2 cups Vegetable Stock
1 cup Cherry Tomatoes (sliced in half or quarters)
1/2 Red Bell Pepper (chopped)
1/2 Green Bell Pepper (chopped)
1/4 cup Red Onion (finly diced)
1/2 Cucumber (diced, approximately 1 cup)
2 tbsps Pesto
1 tbsp Balsamic Vinegar
1 tbsp Lemon Juice (approximately 1/4 lemon)
1 tbsp Balsamic Reduction (optional)

NUTRITION

AMOUNT PER SERVING

Calories	275	Fiber	4g
Fat	7g	Sugar	9g
Carbs	42g	**Protein**	11g

DIRECTIONS

01 Add stock and quinoa to a medium saucepan. Bring to a boil and then reduce heat to low, cover and simmer for about 15 minutes, until tender. Once cooked allow to cool slightly before adding to salad.

02 Combine pesto, lemon juice and balsamic vinegar. Set to the side.

03 Add chopped vegetables and quinoa to a large salad bowl and gently mix until combined.

04 Pour over pesto-balsamic mix and season with salt and pepper.

05 Finish with a drizzle of balsamic reduction (if using).

NOTES

NO QUINOA
Use brown rice instead.
MAIN MEAL SALAD
Serve with boiled eggs, grilled chicken or fish.
STORAGE
Can be kept in the fridge for up to 5 days.
ADD EXTRA FLAVOUR
Add 1/4 cup of crumbled Feta.

Strawberry, Asparagus & Goat's Cheese Salad

4 SERVINGS 10 MINUTES

INGREDIENTS

6 cups Baby Spinach

12 stalks Asparagus (cut into 2" pieces, woody stems removed)

1 cup Strawberries (sliced, stems removed)

1/4 cup Goat Cheese (crumbled)

1/4 cup Slivered Almonds

3 tbsps Extra Virgin Olive Oil

1 tbsp Maple Syrup (or honey)

2 tbsps Lemon Juice

NUTRITION

AMOUNT PER SERVING

Calories	206	Fiber	4g
Fat	16g	Sugar	7g
Carbs	12g	**Protein**	6g

DIRECTIONS

01 In a small bowl combine olive oil, lemon juice, maple syrup and a pinch of salt and pepper. Set to the side.

02 Toss asparagus with 1 tsp of olive oil. Either cook in a large skillet over medium heat for 5-6 minutes or place in a preheated oven (at 400F) and cook for 10 minute.

03 Put the salad together by combining baby spinach, strawberries, sliced almonds, goats cheese and cooked asparagus. Pour over dressing and gently toss.

NOTES

NO BABY SPINACH
Use Arugula or a mixed salad blend.

NO STRAWBERRIES
Substitute for blueberries, grilled peach slices or roasted beets.

Flaked Salmon Salad with Beans and Arugula

2 SERVINGS 15 MINUTES

INGREDIENTS

4 ozs Canned Wild Salmon
1/2 cup Chickpeas
1/2 cup Red Kidney Beans
1/4 Cucumber (sliced)
1/4 cup Radishes (thinly sliced)
4 cups Arugula
2 tbsps Extra Virgin Olive Oil
1 tbsp Lemon (juice)
1 Garlic (crushed)
1/4 cup Parsley (chopped)
1 pinch Sea Salt & Black Pepper (to taste)
1 1/2 tsps Yellow Mustard

NUTRITION

AMOUNT PER SERVING

Calories	354	Fiber	9g
Fat	18g	Sugar	4g
Carbs	25g	**Protein**	24g

DIRECTIONS

01 Make the dressing by combining crushed garlic, lemon juice, mustard and olive oil. Season to taste with salt and pepper.

02 In a bowl toss the cucumber, radish, parsley, chickpeas, kidney beans and arugula and drizzle with the dressing. Divide the salad into portions.

03 Flake the salmon into pieces and place on top of the salad. Serve with additional lemon slices.

NOTES

GRILLED SALMON
Use fresh grilled salmon or Ahi tuna steaks instead of canned salmon.

NO SALMON
Used canned tuna, smoked mackerel, 2 hard boiled eggs/person.

PREP-AHEAD
Make salad and store in an airtight container in the fridge 2-3 day ahead of time. Add dressing and salmon just before serving.

Grilled Salmon and Peach Salad

2 SERVINGS 30 MINUTES

INGREDIENTS

10 ozs Salmon Fillet
1 ear Corn On The Cob
4 cups Mixed Greens
1/2 cup Cherry Tomatoes (halved)
3 tbsps Balsamic Vinegar
1 tbsp Extra Virgin Olive Oil
1 tbsp Soy Sauce Or Tamari (Gf)
1 tbsp Maple Syrup
1/2 tsp Garlic (crushed)
1/4 cup Basil Leaves
1/2 Lemon (cut into wedges)

NUTRITION

AMOUNT PER SERVING

Calories	383	Fiber	2g
Fat	16g	Sugar	14g
Carbs	25g	Protein	33g

DIRECTIONS

01 Preheat oven to 400F.

02 Combine soy sauce, maple syrup, garlic, olive oil and 1/2 of the balsamic vinegar. Place the salmon in a large ziplock bag (or other container) and cover with marinade. Leave to sit in the fridge for 20-30 minutes.

03 Place corn in a pot of boiling water and cook for 5 minutes, remove from water and set aside.

04 Place salmon (skin side down), in a large, preheated skillet. Cook over medium-high heat for 2 minutes. Transfer to a lightly greased baking tray and place in the oven. Cook for 5-7 minutes or until salmon easily flakes apart with a knife.

05 While the salmon is in the oven, add the peach slices and the corn to the skillet the salmon was cooked in. Cook the peaches for 1-2 minute per side and remove. Cook the corn for an extra 2 minutes, turning to achieve a slight charring of the kernels. Remove the corn and slice off the kernels.

06 Pour any remaining marinade back into the skillet and bring to a boil, cook for an additional minute (this will be used as a dressing for the salad).

07 In a large salad bowl, combine green, tomatoes, sliced peaches and corn, gently toss with remaining marinade from the skillet.

08 Finish the salad by adding the salmon. Garnish with fresh basil and lemon.

NOTES

GRILL

Cook the corn, peaches and salmon on a preheated grill or BBQ. Turn corn so each side cooks evenly. Corn will take approximately 10-15 minutes as will the salmon. Grill peaches for 1-2 minutes per side.

Tuna Stack With Fresh Tomato Salsa

2 SERVINGS 5 MINUTES

INGREDIENTS

2 cans Tuna
1 Avocado (diced)
2 Tomato (diced)
1/4 cup Red Onion (finely diced)
1/4 cup Cilantro (chopped)
1 Lime (juice only)
1/4 tsp Chili Flakes (optional)
1/8 tsp Sea Salt & Black Pepper (or more to taste)

DIRECTIONS

01 Combine diced tomato, onion, cilantro, chili flakes, lime juice and salt. For best results do this up to 1 day ahead of time.

02 Divide diced avocado between two bowls, plates or containers, add drained tuna and fresh salsa. Pour remaining juice over top.

NOTES

SERVING SUGGESTIONS

Serve as is or over a bed of shredded lettuce, mixed greens or baby spinach. Use as a topping for tostadas or serve with warm, soft shell tacos.

NUTRITION

AMOUNT PER SERVING

Calories	334	Fiber	8g
Fat	17g	Sugar	2g
Carbs	16g	**Protein**	36g

Buffalo Chicken Salad

4 SERVINGS 35 MINUTES

INGREDIENTS

1 lb Chicken Breast (skinless and boneless, cubed)
1/4 cup Hot Sauce (more or less to taste)
2 ears Corn On The Cob
1 tsp Avocado Oil
2/3 cup Plain Greek Yogurt
3 tbsps Lemon Juice
1 tbsp Honey
1/4 tsp Sea Salt & Black Pepper
1 head Romaine (chopped)
2 Avocado (diced)
2 Tomato (chopped)
2 stalks Green Onion (sliced)

DIRECTIONS

01 Remove the husk from the corn and brush with avocado oil. Cook in a large skillet over medium-high heat rotating every 1 to 2 minutes until lightly charred on all sides. Approximately 8-10 minutes in total. Once cooked, remove and let cool before slicing kernels off the cob.

02 Season chicken with a pinch of salt and pepper. In a large skillet, cook chicken over medium-high heat for 6 to 8 minutes or until no longer pink. Remove chicken and combine with the hot sauce (start with 1/2 the amount of hot sauce listed, then add more to suit your taste).

03 Make the dressing by combining yogurt, lemon juice, raw honey and a pinch of salt and pepper to taste.

04 In a large salad bowl, combine romaine, corn, avocado, tomatoes, chicken and green onion. Gently toss to combine. Drizzle yogurt dressing over top.

NOTES

DIFFERENT DRESSING
Use your favorite dressing to compliment the hot sauce, such as blue cheese or ranch.

MEAL PREP
Prepare the chicken and corn ahead of time. Wash and cut your veggies and make your dressing. Assemble bowls when ready to eat.

NO CORN ON THE COB
Use frozen or canned corn instead.

HOT SAUCE
This recipe was created using Uncle Dougie's Wicked Good No-Fry Wing Marinade.

NUTRITION

AMOUNT PER SERVING

Calories	456	Fiber	10g
Fat	21g	Sugar	7g
Carbs	29g	Protein	44g

Chicken Skewers with Broccoli & Bacon Pasta Salad

4 SERVINGS 25 MINUTES

INGREDIENTS

1 lb Chicken Breast (cut into 1" cubes)
2 slices Bacon (nitrate free)
2 cloves Garlic (crushed)
4 cups Broccoli (cut into florets)
2 cups Cherry Tomatoes (cut into halves)
2 cups Fusilli Pasta (dry measure)
2 cups Baby Spinach (shredded)
1/4 cup Bbq Sauce
1/3 cup Coleslaw Dressing

NUTRITION

AMOUNT PER SERVING

Calories	495	Fiber	5g
Fat	18g	Sugar	15g
Carbs	49g	Protein	36g

DIRECTIONS

01 Thread chicken onto wooden skewers, place in a shallow dish and cover with BBQ sauce (can be done 48 hours ahead of time).

02 Cook pasta as directed on packet. Once cooked drain and rinse under cold water.

03 Cook bacon, remove from pan and place on a paper towel. Once cooled, diced into small pieces.

04 Wipe out any excess fat from the pan and cook the chicken skewers for 4-5 minutes per side or until cooked through.

05 Remove chicken skewers and set to the side. In the same pan add broccoli florets. Cook for 4-5 minutes, add garlic and baby spinach. Cook for an extra 2-3 minutes or until spinach has wilted and broccoli is bright green (and still slightly crunchy).

06 Combine pasta, cooked broccoli & spinach, diced bacon, cherry tomatoes. Toss with coleslaw dressing.

07 Divide salad between plates and place chicken skewers on top.

NOTES

DIFFERENT DRESSING
Use your favorite dressing - Blue Cheese, Caesar, Olive Oil & Balsamic etc.
REDUCE CARBS
Cut pasta by 1/2 and add extra broccoli & tomatoes.
SAVE TIME
Skip the skewers and simply cook the chicken pieces in the hot skillet.

Goats Cheese, Pear & Walnut Salad

2 SERVINGS 10 MINUTES

INGREDIENTS

4 cups Mixed Greens
1/2 Pear (thinly sliced)
1 oz Prosciutto (2 thin slices)
2 tbsps Walnuts (chopped)
2 tbsps Blue Cheese (crumbled)
1 tbsp Extra Virgin Olive Oil
1 tbsp Honey
1/2 tsp Yellow Mustard
1 tsp Lemon Juice
2 tsps Balsamic Reduction

NUTRITION

AMOUNT PER SERVING

Calories	246	Fiber	3g
Fat	15g	Sugar	17g
Carbs	24g	**Protein**	7g

DIRECTIONS

01 In a small bowl combine olive oil, mustard honey and 1 tsp lemon juice. Season with a pinch of salt and pepper. Set aside.

02 In a small bowl toss pear with 1 tsp of lemon juice (this will prevent pear from going brown).

03 In a large salad bowl combine greens, pear, blue cheese, prosciutto and walnuts, gently toss with dressing.

04 Finish with a drizzle of balsamic reduction.

NOTES

NO BLUE CHEESE
Use Goat's cheese, feta or avocado.

NO WALNUTS
Use pecans or pistachio nuts.

Montreal Steak Salad

2 SERVINGS 25 MINUTES

INGREDIENTS

12 ozs Sirloin Tip Steak
1/4 cup Goat Cheese (crumbled)
4 cups Mixed Greens
1 cup Mushrooms (thinly sliced)
1/2 cup Red Onion (thinly sliced, approximately 1/2 onion)
1/2 cup Cherry Tomatoes
1 tbsp Montreal Steak Spice
2 tsps Balsamic Vinegar
1 tsp Yellow Mustard
1 1/2 tbsps Extra Virgin Olive Oil
2 cloves Garlic (crushed)

NUTRITION

AMOUNT PER SERVING

Calories	437	Fiber	2g
Fat	26g	Sugar	5g
Carbs	10g	**Protein**	40g

DIRECTIONS

01 Season steak with Montreal steak spice.

02 Combining olive oil, balsamic vinegar and mustard to make the salad dressing.

03 Preheat skillet to medium-high heat. Add 1 tsp of avocado oil or olive oil, grill steak for 2-3 minutes each side for medium-rare (cook more or less to your liking). Remove from heat and allow to rest for 10 minutes while you put together the salad.

04 In the same pan as the steak was cooked, add garlic, onion and mushrooms, sauté vegetables for 5 minutes . Add 1-2 tbsp of beef broth (or water) during the cooking process - this will help to create a deeper flavor and stop the vegetables from sticking.

05 In a large salad bowl, combine mixed greens, cherry tomatoes and sautéed vegetables. Pour over salad dressing and gently toss. Divide between plates and sprinkle with crumbled Goat's cheese.

06 Thinly slice steak and place on top of salad.

NOTES

NO GOAT'S CHEESE
Use Blue cheese, feta or avocado.

EXTRAS
Add asparagus or Brussel sprouts to the sauté vegetable mix.

NO MONTREAL STEAK SPICE
Use your favorite herbs & spice mix, or simply season with salt and pepper.

NO STEAK
Swap the steak for chicken breast.

Warm Roast Vegetable Salad

4 SERVINGS 40 MINUTES

INGREDIENTS

- **1 lb** Sweet Potato, Orange Flesh (cut into 1" cubes)
- **1** Red Bell Pepper (chopped into large pieces)
- **1** Zucchini (chopped into 1" thick half circles)
- **1** Red Onion (cut into 8 wedges)
- **4 cups** Baby Spinach
- **1/4 cup** Feta Cheese (crumbled)
- **1/4 cup** Plain Yogurt
- **1 tsp** Balsamic Vinegar
- **1/2 tsp** Sea Salt
- **1/2 tsp** Black Pepper
- **1 tsp** Dried Rosemary
- **2 tbsps** Extra Virgin Olive Oil
- **1 tbsp** Balsamic Reduction (optional)
- **6 cloves** Garlic (keep whole)

NUTRITION

AMOUNT PER SERVING

Calories	233	Fiber	5g
Fat	9g	Sugar	12g
Carbs	33g	Protein	6g

DIRECTIONS

01. Preheat oven to 400F.
02. Combine yogurt, crumbled feta and balsamic vinegar. Set aside.
03. Dice sweet potato and place into a microwave safe dish. Cook for 3 minutes.
04. Place garlic cloves on chopping board and with the flat side of a large kitchen knife, give each clove a good 'squish'. You're not chopping them, just crushing the whole clove a little which will help with cooking and distributing flavor (the clove should still be intact, just a bit squished).
05. Place sweet potato, zucchini, red peppers, onion, rosemary and garlic cloves into a deep roasting pan. Add olive oil and mix until vegetables are evenly coated.
06. Cook for 30 minutes, or until vegetables are soft and can easily be pierced with a knife. Stir 1-2 times during cooking.
07. Once vegetables are cooked, stir through baby spinach and yogurt mixture. Spinach will slightly wilt from the heat of the pan and the vegetables. Drizzle with balsamic reduction.

NOTES

WHY THE MICROWAVE?

The key to this salad is sweet potato that is nice and soft. Microwaving the sweet potato for a few minutes ensures that everything cooks at the same time. You can briefly boil the sweet potato if you don't have a microwave.

VEGETABLE COMBINATION

Add any combination of vegetables you like. Add Brussels sprouts, asparagus, cauliflower etc.

Soup, Plant-Based & Fish

Butternut Squash Soup

Creamy Potato & Ham Soup

Minestrone Soup with Meatballs

Mulligatawny Soup

Slow Cooker Thai Chicken Noodle Soup

Jessi's Favorite Toasties

Buddha Bowl with Crispy Tofu

Falafel Bowl

Loaded Fried Rice

Red Lentil Shepherd's Pie

Salmon & Sweet Potato Cakes

Lentil Patties

Zucchini & Corn Fritters

Butternut Squash Soup

6 SERVINGS 1 HOUR

INGREDIENTS

8 cups Butternut Squash (approximately 2 lbs peeled, seeds removed and chopped)
1 Yellow Onion (chopped)
2 stalks Celery
2 Carrot (chopped)
1 tbsp Ginger (peeled and grated)
1 tsp Curry Powder (optional)
6 cups Vegetable Broth
1/2 tsp Sea Salt
1/4 cup Heavy Cream (optional)

NUTRITION

AMOUNT PER SERVING

Calories	148	Fiber	5g
Fat	4g	Sugar	8g
Carbs	28g	Protein	3g

DIRECTIONS

01 Sauté onion, carrots and celery for 3-4 minutes or until they begin to soften.

02 Add diced butternut squash, ginger and curry powder, cook for 10 minutes on low heat. Add a little vegetable broth if the veggies begin to stick on the bottom.

03 Add broth, bring to a boil, cover and reduce heat to a simmer. Simmer for 20-25 minutes.

04 Use an immersion blender to puree the soup. Serve with a little swirl of cream (if using).

NOTES

LEFTOVERS
Refrigerate in an airtight container for 4-5 days. Freeze for up to 3 months.
SAVE TIME
Use pre-sliced butternut squash cubes (fresh or frozen).
OPTIONAL TOPPINGS
Roasted pumpkin or squash seeds, plain yogurt, coconut cream, or cilantro.
NO VEGETABLE BROTH
Use bone broth or chicken broth instead.

Potato & Ham Soup

6 SERVINGS 40 MINUTES

INGREDIENTS

1/2 Onion (finely diced)
2 Carrot (diced)
2 stalks Celery (diced)
2 Russet Potato (scrubbed & diced, approximately 3 cups)
1 cup Cooked Ham (diced, add more if desired)
3 cups Water
1 tbsp Chicken Stock Concentrate
2 cups Milk (or plant based milk)
2 1/2 tbsps Corn Starch
1/4 tsp Sea Salt (adjust to taste, if needed)
1/2 tsp Black Pepper

NUTRITION

AMOUNT PER SERVING

Calories	199	Fiber	2g
Fat	3g	Sugar	6g
Carbs	27g	Protein	13g

DIRECTIONS

01 Place onion, carrot, celery, potatoes, water and diced ham in a large stockpot. Bring to a boil and then reduce heat to a simmer. Cooker for 10-15 minutes or until potatoes are tender.

02 Add milk (reserving 1/4 cup) and chicken stock concentrate, stir well.

03 Mix corn flour with remaining milk until it forms a smooth paste. Pour into the soup and continue cooking until soup thickens.

04 Taste soup and adjust flavor with salt and pepper if needed.

05 Allow to cool slightly before serving.

NOTES

NO CHICKEN STOCK CONCENTRATE
Use 1 Tbsp. chicken bouillon granules or use 3 cups chicken stock instead of the 3 cups of water.

VEGETARAIN
Skip the ham and add 1 cup sautéed mushrooms. Use vegetable stock instead of the chicken stock and use a plant based milk.

NO HAM
Add cooked, diced chicken or cod.

KEEP THE SKIN
You can leave the skin on the potatoes and carrots, just make sure you give them a good scrub first.

Mulligatawny Soup

6 SERVINGS 30 MINUTES

INGREDIENTS

1 tsp Coconut Oil
1 lb Chicken Thighs (boneless, skinless, chopped)
1 Onion (medium, chopped)
2 stalks Celery (sliced)
1 Sweet Potato (cut into cubes, approximately 3 cups)
1 Carrot (large, chopped)
1 Green Apple (peeled and chopped)
1 tsp Ginger (grated)
2 cloves Garlic (crushed)
1/2 cup Canned Coconut Milk
6 cups Stock (chicken or vegetable)
1/2 tsp Turmeric
1 tsp Garam Masala
1 tbsp Curry Powder (yellow and mild)
1 Bay Leaf
1/2 cup Basmati Rice
1/4 cup Cilantro (optional, for topping, chopped)

NUTRITION

AMOUNT PER SERVING

Calories	268	Fiber	3g
Fat	8g	Sugar	6g
Carbs	27g	**Protein**	22g

DIRECTIONS

01 Cook rice as directed on packet.

02 In a large pot over medium heat, add oil and diced chicken. Sauté until lightly brown and just cooked through. Set aside and return pot to heat.

03 Add an extra tsp of coconut oil to the pot. Add onions, carrot, celery, ginger and garlic, sauté, scraping up any brown bits on the bottom of the pan, 3-4 minutes.

04 Add curry powder, Garam Masala and turmeric, cook for 30-60 seconds. Add chicken back to the pot along with diced sweet potato, Bay leaf and stock. Bring to a boil and then reduce to simmer.

05 Simmer for 10 minutes and then add diced apple. Continue to simmer for another 10 minutes or until sweet potatoes are tender.

06 Stir through cooked rice and coconut milk, cook for an additional 2-3 minutes. Remove Bay leaf, season with additional salt and pepper if needed. Serve with cilantro (if using).

NOTES

LEFTOVERS
Refrigerate in an airtight container for up to three days. Or freeze for up to 3 months.

VEGETARIAN
Instead of chicken add 2 cups of cooked red lentils. Or 1 cup of dry lentils plus an additional 1.5cups of stock.

NO SWEET POTATO
Use diced russet potatoes or butternut squash instead.

MAKE IT CREAMIER
Reduce stock to 5.5 cups and increase coconut milk to 1 cup.

THICKER TEXTURE
Before you add the chicken back in, remove 2 cups of the soup mixture. Puree in a blender and then stir back into the soup before you add the chicken.

Minestrone Soup with Meatballs

6 SERVINGS 40 MINUTES

INGREDIENTS

1 White Onion (diced)
2 Carrot (diced)
1 stalk Celery (diced)
1 Zucchini (small, diced- approximately 1/2 cup)
1 cup Green Cabbage (shredded)
1 tin Diced Tomatoes (28oz/796ml)
4 cups Chicken Broth
1 cup Tomato Sauce (look for Passata or substitute with pureed tomatoes)
1 tsp Dried Basil
1 Sea Salt & Black Pepper (to season)
1 lb Italian Sausages (fresh)
1 cup Red Kidney Beans
1 cup Rotini Pasta
3 tbsps Parmesan Cheese

NUTRITION

AMOUNT PER SERVING

Calories	494	Fiber	11g	
Fat	17g	Sugar	21g	
Carbs	56g	Protein	27g	

DIRECTIONS

01 Cook pasta for 2-3 minutes less than directed on packet. The pasta will absorb some of the liquid from the soup so you don't want to over cook it. Drain and set aside until needed.

02 Squeeze the sausage meat out of the casings, making small meatballs. Brown meatballs in a large pot. Remove once cooked.

03 Add onion, carrots and celery to the same pot and cook for 3-4 minutes until they begin to soften.

04 Add zucchini, cabbage and dried herbs, cook for another 2-3 minutes.

05 Place meatballs back into the pot, add stock, diced tomatoes and tomato sauce (passata sauce). Bring to a boil and then reduce heat to low, cover and simmer for 15 minutes.

06 Add pasta and continue to cook for another 5 minutes before serving.

07 Divide soup between bowls and top with Parmesan cheese.

NOTES

VEGETARIAN VERSION
Swap sausage for vegetarian sausage or increase red kidney beans to 3 cups.

MEAL PREP
Chop onion, carrot, celery & zucchini ahead of time. Cook sausage and pasta up to 4 days in advance.

GLUTEN FREE
When using gluten free pasta, cook pasta and set aside. Add pasta to the bowl and pour soup over top. GF pasta will become VERY soft if left in the soup. It's better to keep them separate and simply combine when ready to eat.

Slow Cooker Thai Chicken Noodle Soup

6 SERVINGS 3 HOURS

INGREDIENTS

1 lb Chicken Breast
3 cups Lite Coconut Milk (2 x 14oz can)
1/4 cup Peanut Butter
2 tbsps Thai Red Curry Paste (or more depending how spicy you like it)
3 cups Chicken Broth
1/4 cup Soy Sauce Or Tamari (Gf)
1 tbsp Fish Sauce
2 tbsps Brown Sugar
4 Garlic (crushed)
1 tbsp Ginger (fresh, grated)
1 Onion (finly diced)
1 Red Bell Pepper (thinly sliced)
1 Carrot (thinly sliced)
3 cups Broccoli (cut into small florrets)
1 Lime
1/4 cup Cilantro (or Thai Basil)
2 cups Vermicelli Rice Noodles

NUTRITION

AMOUNT PER SERVING

Calories	371	Fiber	4g
Fat	16g	Sugar	11g
Carbs	33g	Protein	25g

DIRECTIONS

01 In a large bowl whisk together coconut milk, chicken broth, peanut butter, soy sauce, fish sauce, curry paste, garlic and ginger.

02 Place chicken at the base of slow cooker, add onion, carrots, peppers and broccoli florets.

03 Carefully pour sauce mixture over top. Cook on low for 5-6 hours or high for 3-4 hours.

04 Remove chicken from slow cooker (when it reaches an internal temperature of 165F), dice or shred chicken. Return chicken to slow cooker, add juice from 1/2 lime. Stir and cook for another 5-10 minutes. Taste and season with additional salt if needed.

05 Cook vermicelli noodles as directed on packet. Set to the side until ready to use.

06 To serve, divide noodles between bowls and cover with soup. Garnish with fresh cilantro, a lime wedge and crushed peanuts (optional).

NOTES

VEGETARIAN

Use Vegetable broth instead of chicken broth. Swap chicken for 1 block of firm tofu (cubed). Cook on high for 1.5-2.5 hours or on low for 3-4 hours.

Jessi's Favourite Toasties

4 SERVINGS 20 MINUTES

INGREDIENTS

4 slices Whole Grain Bread
1/2 cup Baked Beans
1 Egg (lightly beaten)
1/4 cup Yellow Onion (diced)
1/2 cup Cheddar Cheese (grated)
1 Tomato (small, diced)
1/2 tsp Garlic (crushed)

NUTRITION

AMOUNT PER SERVING

Calories	212	**Fiber**	4g
Fat	8g	**Sugar**	4g
Carbs	24g	**Protein**	12g

DIRECTIONS

01 Preheat oven to 350F.

02 Use the bagel setting on your toaster and toast 1 side of each piece of bread (use the grill setting in your oven if you don't have a bagel setting on your toaster).

03 Combine the egg, garlic, onion, diced tomato, grated cheese and baked beans (drain as much sauce from the beans as possible).

04 Place the bread, cooked side down, on a baking tray and divide the bean mix between the slices.

05 Bake in the oven for 20-25 minutes or until egg is cooked through.

NOTES

SERVE WITH
Your favorite soup (or prep ahead for a grab-and-go breakfast option).

ADD FRESH HERBS
Add fresh parsley, chives or green onion.

SPICY
Add some chili flakes or a splash of your favorite hot sauce.

EXTRA PROTEIN
Add some sliced ham or cooked diced chicken.

AVOCADO
For a little bit of extra deliciousness, add some diced avocado to the mix.

Buddha Bowl with Crispy Tofu

2 SERVINGS 25 MINUTES

INGREDIENTS

8 ozs Tofu (extra firm cut into 1" cubes)
2 tbsps Corn Starch
1/2 tsp Sea Salt & Black Pepper
1/2 tsp Garlic Powder
1/2 cup Quinoa
1 Carrot (large, shredded)
1/2 Beet (grated)
1/2 Avocado
1 Spicy Satay Peanut Sauce (recipe on page 73)
1 tbsp Coconut Oil
1/2 cup Frozen Edamame

NUTRITION

AMOUNT PER SERVING

Calories	492	Fiber	11g
Fat	25g	Sugar	5g
Carbs	49g	Protein	24g

DIRECTIONS

01 Rinse quinoa and cook as directed on packet.
02 In a small bowl combine corn starch, salt, pepper and garlic powder. Add diced tofu and toss until evenly coated.
03 Heat oil in a large skillet over medium-high heat. Cook tofu until crispy, turning often so that each side cooks evenly and turns golden brown.
04 Divide cooked quinoa and prepared vegetables between 2 bowls.
05 Divide tofu between bowls and drizzle with warm, spicy peanut sauce.
06 Cook edamame as directed on packet.

NOTES

NO TOFU
Use grilled chicken or shrimp.

ADDITIONAL TOPPINGS
Add hemp seeds, sesame seeds, fresh cilantro or other herb or fresh sliced chili peppers. Use any combination of vegetables you like.

SAVE TIME
Use pre made peanut sauce or choose one of your own favorites.

NO QUINOA
Use rice or noodles instead.

Falafel Bowl

4 SERVINGS 20 MINUTES

INGREDIENTS

1 box Falafel Mix (make 4/person)
3/4 cup Quinoa
1 Red Onion (sliced)
16 stalks Asparagus
1/2 cup Feta Cheese (crumbled)
1 Beet (raw, grated)
1 Red Bell Pepper (sliced)
1/2 cup Baba Ganoush (eggplant dip)
2 tbsps Avocado Oil
1 Lemon (quartered)
1 tsp Dijon Mustard
1 1/2 tsps Extra Virgin Olive Oil
1 tbsp Red Wine Vinegar
1/4 cup Flat Leaf Parsley (fresh, chopped, loosley packed)

NUTRITION

AMOUNT PER SERVING

Calories	487	Fiber	14g
Fat	19g	Sugar	5g
Carbs	61g	Protein	19g

DIRECTIONS

01 Make falafels as directed on packet (this may need to be done 1-2 hours ahead of time depending on brand).

02 Cook quinoa as directed on packet.

03 In a small bowl mix together olive oil, Dijon mustard, vinegar and chopped parsley. Season with salt and pepper. Set aside.

04 Peel and grate beet, toss with olive oil, Dijon dressing.

05 Heat a large skillet, add 1 tsp oil and cook the onion and pepper for 5 mins then add in the asparagus and cook for another 3-4 mins. Season with salt and pepper.

06 Heat the remaining oil in a frying pan, cook the falafels for 4 minutes each side (or as directed on packet) until golden brown.

07 To assemble, divide quinoa between bowls, top with grilled veggies, falafels & beetroot. Serve with eggplant dip, crumble feta and a wedge of lemon.

NOTES

FALAFELS
This recipe & nutrition facts were created using: Nature's Earthly Choice - Original Quinoa & Falafel mix.

PREP AHEAD
Falafels can be prepped and cooked 4 days ahead of use. Beets can be prepped 1-2 days ahead of time (they actually taste better when they've marinated for at least an hour).

KID FRIENDLY TIPS
Keep the bowls simple for kids and add some sliced pita bread and raw veggies for dipping in the hummus and Baba ganoush.

VEGETABELS
Use and combination or additional vegetables.

SOFTER FALAFALS
Combine 1/2 cup mashed potatoes (regular or sweet) to create a 'softer' falafel mix.

NO QUINOA
Serve with rice, couscous or baby greens.

Loaded Fried Rice with Vegetables

4 SERVINGS 20 MINUTES

INGREDIENTS

3/4 cup Jasmine Rice (dry measure)
1 cup Frozen Edamame (cooked)
2 Egg (lightly beaten)
1/4 head Cauliflower (diced)
2 Carrot (diced)
1 White Onion (diced)
1 cup Broccoli (diced)
1/2 Red Bell Pepper (diced)
1 tsp Garlic (crushed)
1/4 cup Soy Sauce Or Tamari (Gf)
1/2 tsp Sesame Oil
1/2 cup Roasted Peanuts
2 tsps Oyster Sauce (optional)
1 tbsp Avocado Oil
2 stalks Green Onion

NUTRITION

AMOUNT PER SERVING

Calories	399	Fiber	8g
Fat	18g	Sugar	7g
Carbs	46g	**Protein**	19g

DIRECTIONS

01 Cook rice as directed on packet. For best results, allow to cool completely (you can cook the rice up to 5 days ahead of time).

02 Cook edamame as directed on packet.

03 In a small pan, scramble egg with a small amount of butter. Mover the egg around breaking into small pieces. Once cooked, set aside.

04 Heat a small amount of oil in a large wok or skillet. Add onion and garlic, cook for 2 minutes. Add diced carrots, peppers, broccoli and cauliflower, continue to cook until vegetables are just beginning to soften, approximately 5 minutes.

05 Move vegetables to the side (as much as possible) add remaining oil, allow to heat up for 20-30 seconds. Turn up heat to high, add rice, soy sauce, oyster sauce (if using) and green onion. 'Fry' the rice for 3-4 minutes, stirring continuously.

06 Add in egg and edamame, stir to combine. Remove from heat, add sesame oil and gently stir until combined.

07 Serve with roasted peanuts.

NOTES

SERVING OPTIONS
Serve as is for a main meal, or as a side with grilled chicken, shrimp, tofu or beef skewers.

VEGETABLES
Use any combination of vegetables that you have on hand.

MAKE IT SPICY
Add your favorite hot sauce.

FEEDING KIDS
Remove a portion of the fried rice (that you are going to serve to your kids) and in a separate pan melt 1 tbsp peanut butter and 1 tsp honey. Add the fried rice and mix until well combined. My kids love 'PB Fried rice' :)

Red Lentil Shepherd's Pie

4 SERVINGS 1 HOUR 10 MINUTES

INGREDIENTS

1 cup Dry Red Lentils
2 cups Vegetable Broth
2 Sweet Potato (chopped, approximately 4 cups)
2 Garlic (cloves, crushed)
1 White Onion (chopped)
2 Carrot (chopped)
1 cup Mushrooms (sliced)
2 stalks Celery (diced)
8 ozs Creamed Corn (small tin)
1/2 cup Frozen Peas
2 tbsps Nutritional Yeast (optional)
1/4 cup Milk Of Choice
1 tbsp Extra Virgin Olive Oil
1 tsp Soy Sauce Or Tamari (Gf)
2 tsps Worcestershire Sauce
1 tsp Dried Rosemary
1 tsp Oregano (dried)
1 Bay Leaf
1 lb Green Beans
1 tbsp Corn Starch

NUTRITION

AMOUNT PER SERVING

Calories	402	Fiber	16g
Fat	5g	Sugar	11g
Carbs	74g	Protein	20g

DIRECTIONS

01 Preheat oven to 400F.

02 Rinse lentils and place in a large pot with vegetable stock. Bring to a boil, reduce heat and simmer for 10-15 minutes with the lid on.

03 Steam sweet potatoes until soft. Add half the milk and nutritional yeast, mash until smooth adding a little more milk if needed. Season with salt and pepper.

04 Heat oil in a large skillet. Add onion, garlic, celery, carrots and mushrooms. Saute for 10 minutes or until vegetables are very soft and beginning to brown on the edges.

05 Add lentils, creamed corn, dried herbs, soy sauce and Worcestershire. Simmer uncovered for 10 minutes.

06 If mixture is too 'thin', combine corn starch with 2 tbsp. water and stir into a slurry. Stir through red lentil mixture and continue to cook for 2-3 minutes until thickened.

07 Pour mixture into a large oven proof dish, cover with mashed sweet potatoes. Bake for 30 minutes or until potatoes are golden.

08 Remove from oven and allow to sit for 10 minutes before serving.

09 Serve with steamed green beans.

NOTES

TIME SAVERS

Instead of dry lentils, use 1 can of seasoned pre-cooked lentils.

MAKE IT CHEESY

Add 1/2 cup grated cheddar cheese or 2-3 Tbsp. grated Parmesan cheese (or both) to the mashed sweet potato.

Salmon and Sweet Potato Cakes

4 SERVINGS 30 MINUTES

INGREDIENTS

1 1/2 lbs Sweet Potatoes (scrubbed, diced)
14 ozs Canned Wild Salmon
2 Egg (lightly beaten)
1/2 cup Gluten Free Bread Crumbs (plus extra if needed)
2 stalks Green Onion (finely chopped)
1 1/2 tbsps Seafood Seasoning (Old Bay)
1 tsp Lemon Zest

NUTRITION

AMOUNT PER SERVING

Calories	470	Fiber	7g
Fat	12g	Sugar	8g
Carbs	56g	**Protein**	34g

DIRECTIONS

01 Steam sweet potatoes until they are soft (alternatively, place in a microwave dish with 2 tbsp water, cover and cook for 8-10 minutes). Mash until smooth and allow to cool.

02 In a large bowl beat egg, add salmon and flake with a fork, add mashed sweet potato, seasoning, green onion, lemon zest and ½ the bread crumbs. Mix to combine. The mixture needs to be firm enough to form into patties, add a little more bread crumbs if the mixture is too wet.

03 Scoop 1/3 cup of the mixture and form into a pattie. Repeat.

04 Add the remaining bread crumbs to a shallow dish and gently press each patty into the bread crumbs - press down gently to coat each side. Use additional breadcrumbs if needed. For best results allow to sit in the fridge for at least 1 hour or overnight before cooking.

05 In a large skillet heat 2 tbsp avocado oil over medium-high heat. Cook salmon patties for 4-5 minutes per side or until golden brown.

06 Serve with a mixed salad or a side of steamed vegetables.

NOTES

NO SALMON
Used canned tuna instead.

PREP AHEAD
Prep the salmon cakes up to 4 days ahead of time.

FREEZER SAFE
Can be pre-made and kept in the freezer. Separate with parchment paper and add 2 tbsp of extra bread crumbs to the mix before forming the salmon cakes.

ADD HERBS
Use fresh dill, chives, flat leaf parsley or cilantro.

Lentil Patties

4 SERVINGS 30 MINUTES

INGREDIENTS

2 1/2 cups Cooked Lentils (or canned)
1 cup Quick Oats
2 Egg
1 Carrot (grated)
1/2 cup White Onion (diced)
2 Garlic (cloves, crushed)
1/3 cup Parsley (optional)
2 tbsps Soy Sauce Or Tamari (Gf)
1 tsp Cumin
1 tsp Oregano
1 Pinch Salt And Pepper (to taste)
2 tbsps Avocado Oil

NUTRITION

AMOUNT PER SERVING

Calories	340	Fiber	13g
Fat	11g	Sugar	4g
Carbs	44g	Protein	18g

DIRECTIONS

01 Add cooked lentils to a food processor and pulse on low speed for 20-30 seconds until a rough paste forms, leaving a few lentils intact for texture.

02 Add all other ingredients to the food processor. Mix for 30-60 seconds on low speed until well combined.

03 Use a 1/3 measuring cup and scoop out portions of the mixture. Form into patties using your hands. Let the patties 'rest' in the fridge for at least 30 minutes. The longer they rest the firmer they become making them easier to cook.

04 Heat a large skillet over medium-high heat and add 2 tbsp oil. Cook patties for 5 minutes on each side or until they become golden brown. Serve with a large green salad or a vegetable side dish.

NOTES

PREP-AHEAD
Prep up to 4 days ahead.
FREEZER
Once cooked, store in freezer for up to 4 months. Separate each pattie with parchment paper.
NO FOOD PROCESSOR
Place lentils in a large bowl and mash with the back of a spoon. Patties will still stay together, the texture will just be a little more chunky.
VEGAN
Substitute egg with 2TBSP ground flax and 6 TBSP warm water. Combine flax and water and stir well, allow to sit for 5 minutes before using.

Zucchini & Corn Fritters

4 SERVINGS 40 MINUTES

INGREDIENTS

2 Zucchini (large, grated)
1/2 cup Corn
1/2 Yellow Onion (finly diced)
1 clove Garlic (crushed)
2 Egg
1/4 cup Plain Greek Yogurt
1/2 cup All Purpose Gluten Free Flour (or regular flour)
1/2 tsp Baking Soda
2 tbsps Ground Flax Seed
Avocado Oil (for cooking)
1 tsp Sea Salt
2 stalks Green Onions (chopped)

NUTRITION

AMOUNT PER SERVING

Calories	176	Fiber	6g
Fat	4g	Sugar	5g
Carbs	27g	**Protein**	8g

DIRECTIONS

01 Sprinkle grated zucchini with salt. Allow to sit for 10 minutes. Wrap zucchini in a kitchen towel and squeeze out as much liquid as possible.

02 Combine yogurt and egg in a large bowl. Mix in zucchini, corn, ground flax, green onion, garlic and diced onion. Sprinkle in flour and baking soda, combine well. Season with salt and pepper.

03 Heat oil in a large pan over medium heat. Scoop 1/4 cup of the mixture and place in the hot pan. Cook for 2 to 3 minutes per side and transfer to a plate lined with paper towel.

04 Serve with a mixed green salad or steamed vegetables.

NOTES

OVEN BAKED
Scoop onto a parchment-lined baking sheet and bake in the oven for 20 to 25 minutes at 375F.

ADJUST THE MIXTRUE
If the mixture is too runny, add 1 tbsp flour at a time until you reach the right consistency.

MAKE THEM CHEESY
Add 1/2 cup grated cheese to the mixture.

Chicken & Turkey

Buffalo Chicken Bites

Grilled Fish Tacos

Instant Pot

Instant Pot Mini Meatloaf

Quiche

Quick & Easy Chicken Tostadas

Prosciutto Wrapped Stuffed Chicken Breast

Sheet Pan Chicken Fajitas

Sheet Pan Mini Meat Loaf with Vegetables

Sheet Pan Pesto Chicken & Grilled Vegetables

Buffalo Chicken Bites

4 SERVINGS 30 MINUTES

INGREDIENTS

1 lb Chicken Breast (cut into bite size pieces)
1/4 cup Plain Yogurt
3 cups Cornflake
1/4 cup All Purpose Gluten Free Flour
1/2 tsp Paprika
1/4 tsp Sea Salt
1/2 tsp Black Pepper
2 tbsps Hot Sauce (your favourite brand)
2 tbsps Bbq Sauce (your favourite brand)
1 tbsp Butter (melted)
1/4 cup Avocado Oil

NUTRITION

AMOUNT PER SERVING

Calories	421	Fiber	2g
Fat	20g	Sugar	6g
Carbs	31g	Protein	28g

DIRECTIONS

01 Place chicken in a large bowl, season with salt, pepper and paprika. Pour in yogurt and mix until chicken is well coated. Can be done up to 24 hours ahead.

02 Place corn flakes into a food processor. Blitz until you get 'panko' sized bread crumbs, add flour and blitz one more time for 10 seconds. Pour out into a shallow dish.

03 Working with 3-4 pieces at a time, dip chicken into bread crumbs to evenly coat. Press down gently to make sure the breadcrumbs stick. Repeat until all chicken is coated.

04 Over medium/high heat, add avocado oil to a large skillet. Once oil is hot, add chicken pieces and cook for 4-5 minutes per side until golden brown and cooked through.

05 Combine melted butter, hot sauce and BBQ sauce in a large bowl. Add cooked chicken pieces and gently toss, to evenly coat chicken.

06 Serve with raw veggies and your favorite dipping sauce.

NOTES

MEAL PREP
Chicken can marinade in yogurt for up to 24 hours - any longer and the yogurt can begin to 'over' tenderize the chicken.

MAKE IT HOT HOT
Add jerk seasoning or cayenne pepper to the cornflake crumbs.

NO CORN FLAKES
Use regular bread crumbs.

GLUTEN FREE
Make sure that your cornflakes are gluten free (some cornflakes contain barley malt). Nature's Path Corn Flakes were used in his recipe.

Chicken Enchiladas

6 SERVINGS 40 MINUTES

INGREDIENTS

1 lb Chicken Breast (cut into 1/4" strips)
1 White Onion (diced)
1 Red Bell Pepper (diced)
1 cup Frozen Corn
1 cup Black Beans
2 tbsps Taco Seasoning Mix (page 81)
1 cup Salsa
6 Whole Grain Wraps
6 ozs Cheddar Cheese (grated)
1 tin Diced Tomatoes (14oz/400ml - with chili peppers if you like it hot)
1/2 can Refried Beans (3/4 cup)
Cilantro & Lime (Optional)

DIRECTIONS

01 Preheat oven to 375F. Lightly grease a 13x19 baking dish.

02 In a large skillet sauté onion and peppers for 2 minutes. Add chicken and cook until chicken is no longer pink.

03 Add corn, black beans and taco seasoning. Cook until spices release their fragrance (1-2 minutes).

04 Pour in diced tomatoes and stir through refried beans. Bring to a boil and then reduce heat, simmer for 10 minutes.

05 Lay the tortilla wraps out and scoop 1/6 of the mixture on to the tortilla. Roll up and place seam-side down in the baking tray. Repeat until all done. If there is any mixture left, spread it over top of the wraps.

06 Pour salsa evenly over the wraps and sprinkle with cheese.

07 Bake for 20 minutes or until sauce is bubbling and cheese is melted. Serve with fresh cilantro and lime.

NOTES

SAVE TIME
Use pre-cooked chicken. Chop into small cubes and add to the sautéed vegetables.
GLUTEN FREE
Use gluten free wraps.
LOW CARB VERSION
Use large Swiss chard leaves or cabbage leaves instead of whole grain wraps.
ALTERNATIVES
Instead of chicken breast us ground chicken, ground beef, pulled pork (recipe 108) or create a vegetarian meal by using 1 packet of Yves Veggie Ground Round (or other plant based brand) or simply add 2 cups of rinsed and drained canned beans.

Chicken Pot Pie

4 SERVINGS 1 HOUR

INGREDIENTS

1 lb Chicken Breast (cut into 1/2" cubes)
1 Onion (diced)
1 Carrot (diced)
2 stalks Celery (diced)
1/2 cup Frozen Peas
1/2 cup Frozen Corn
1 cup Chicken Broth
1 cup Milk (of choice, unsweetened)
2 tbsps Corn Starch
1 tsp Poultry Seasoning
1/2 tsp Sea Salt
1/2 tsp Black Pepper
1 clove Garlic (crushed)
1 sheet Puff Pastry (frozen, pre-rolled, ready to bake. Try Tenderflake.)
1 tbsp Extra Virgin Olive Oil
1 Egg (lightly beaten)

NUTRITION

AMOUNT PER SERVING

Calories	309	Fiber	6g
Fat	22g	Sugar	9g
Carbs	42g	Protein	34g

DIRECTIONS

01 Pre-heat oven to 400F.

02 In a large skillet add olive oil and saute onion, garlic, chicken, carrots, celery for 5-7 minutes or until chicken is cooked through.

03 Add frozen peas and carrots. Stir in shredded or diced (cooked) chicken, poultry spice, salt and pepper. Stir for 1 minute.

04 Add chicken broth and milk. Bring to a boil and then reduce heat.

05 Mix corn starch in a small bowl with 2-3 tbsp. of chicken broth until completely smooth. Slowly pour into chicken mixture and stir until thickened, 3-5 minutes.

06 Pour mixture into an oven safe casserole dish, top with puff pastry. Dip a pastry brush in the beaten egg and brush the pastry all over (this will help the top to go nice and brown).

07 Cook for 25-30 minutes until golden brown and bubbling. Allow to sit for 5-10 minutes before serving.

08 Serve with steamed broccolini, green beans or a garden salad.

NOTES

NUTRITION INFOMATION
Nutrition information is based on using Tenderflake Puff Pastry. Other brands may change the nutrition information.

SAVE TIME
Use 1 cup of frozen pre-cut vegetables instead of the carrot and onion. Keep the fresh celery as it provides that classic chicken pot pie flavor.

CURRY TWIST
Add 1 tsp of Keen's Curry powder when adding the poultry spice.

VEGETARIAN
Swap the chicken for a cup of sautéed mushrooms and 1 1/2 cups chickpeas.

COOKED CHICKEN
Save time by using rotisserie chicken or left over, pre-cooked chicken.

NO PASTRY
Instead of pastry, use 2 cups mashed sweet potato with 1/2 cup grated cheddar (optional) mix in.

Cilantro Lime Chicken

4 SERVINGS 30 MINUTES

INGREDIENTS

1 lb Chicken Thighs
1 tbsp Avocado Oil
2 tsps Garlic (crushed)
1/2 Lime (juice)
1/4 cup Plain Yogurt
1/2 cup Cilantro (chopped, loosely packed)
1/2 tsp Paprika
1/2 tsp Sea Salt & Black Pepper

NUTRITION

AMOUNT PER SERVING

Calories	179	Fiber		0g
Fat	8g	Sugar		1g
Carbs	1g	Protein		23g

DIRECTIONS

01 Place yogurt, avocado oil, garlic, cilantro, paprika, lime juice, salt and pepper into a food processor. Pulse until well combined.

02 Place chicken in a zip lock bag or a glass container, cover with marinade. Refrigerate and allow to marinade for 1-24 hours

03 Heat oven broil/grill setting to high. Place chicken on a baking tray lined with foil and place under the broil. Cook for 5 minutes per side (or until internal temperature reaches 165).

NOTES

SERVING SUGGESTION
Serve with jasmine rice and steamed vegetables. Use chicken in tacos, wraps or as part of a burrito bowl. Serve with boiled corn and a mixed salad.

PREP AHEAD
Chicken can be prepped up to 24 hours ahead.

NO OVEN BROIL/GRILL SETTING
Cook chicken in a large skillet over medium-high heat for 5-7 minutes per side. Or grill on an outside BBQ.

Deconstructed Chicken Parmigiana

4 SERVINGS 30 MINUTES

INGREDIENTS

1 lb Chicken Thighs (boneless, skinless)
1 tin Diced Tomatoes (28oz/796ml, drained)
1 cup Pasta Sauce (your favourite brand - see notes)
2 cloves Garlic (crushed)
1/2 cup Onion (diced)
1 tsp Italian Seasoning
4 slices Whole Grain Bread
1/4 cup Parsley (chopped)
1 1/2 tbsps Extra Virgin Olive Oil
2 tbsps Parmesan Cheese
4 ozs Mozzarella Cheese (grated)
1 lb Green Beans

NUTRITION

AMOUNT PER SERVING

Calories	434	Fiber	10g
Fat	18g	Sugar	8g
Carbs	39g	**Protein**	38g

NOTES

GLUTEN FREE
Use gluten free bread.
REDUCE THE FAT
Use chicken breast instead of chicken thigh.
ADD EXTRA VEGETABLES
Sauté sliced zucchini and diced bell peppers with the onion.
PASTA SAUCE
This recipe was developed and tested using Newman's Marinara Pasta Sauce

DIRECTIONS

01 Preheat oven to 400F.

02 In a food processor combine bread, parsley and Parmesan cheese. Process until small bread crumbs form. Add 1 tbsp olive oil, process for another 30 seconds. Set aside.

03 Sauté onion and garlic until soft, pour in pasta sauce, drained tomatoes and Italian seasoning, mix well.

04 Place chicken into the 13" x 9" casserole dish. Pour diced tomato mix over chicken. pSrinkle mozzarella cheese over each chicken piece and then cover everything evenly with bread crumbs.

05 Bake for 30 minutes (or until chicken reaches 165F). If breadcrumbs begin to go too brown, cover with tin foil until finished cooking.

06 Allow to chicken to cool down for 5 minutes before serving. Steam green beans (or other vegetables) while chicken is cooling.

Fresh Summer Rolls

4 SERVINGS 30 MINUTES

INGREDIENTS

12 ozs Chicken Breast, Cooked (diced)
2 tbsps Soy Sauce Or Tamari (Gf)
1 tsp Sriracha Sauce (or more to taste)
1/2 cup Cilantro
1 Lime (juice half and cut the other half into wedges)
12 Rice Paper Wraps
1/2 Cucumber (sliced into thin strips)
1 Red Bell Pepper (thinly sliced)
2 Carrot (grated)
2 cups Mixed Greens
1 Peanut Satay Sauce (recipe on following page)

NUTRITION

AMOUNT PER SERVING

Calories	243	Fiber	2g
Fat	2g	Sugar	4g
Carbs	34g	Protein	21g

DIRECTIONS

01 In a small bowl combine soy sauce (or Tamari), lime juice, sriracha sauce, cilantro and diced/shredded chicken. Gently combine.

02 Slice and prepare vegetables.

03 Add hot water to a shallow skillet. Place a rice paper wrap in the water to soften (about 10 seconds). Do not submerge for too long or the rice paper wrap will become too difficult to work with. Transfer to a clean surface.

04 Add cucumber, pepper, grated carrot, leafy greens and chicken on one side of the rice wrap (the same way you would if making a burrito). Fold the top over the filling, fold the sides in and then roll the rice paper until completely wrapped. Transfer to a plate. Repeat this process until all ingredients are used up.

05 Serve with a side of spicy peanut sauce.

NOTES

VEGETARIAN
Use strips of marinated tofu or tempeh.

STORAGE
Store in the fridge in an airtight container for up to 2 days (but these are best served fresh).

ADDITIONAL FILLINGS
Add sliced mango, avocado, rice noodles, sprouts, grated beet - or any of your other favorites.

NO RICE WRAPS
Use nori sheets, Swiss chard or collard greens as wraps.

PRACTICE
The more you practice the better you will become at rolling the wrap and you will be able to prepare multiple wraps at a time.

Spicy Peanut Sauce

8 SERVINGS 10 MINUTES

INGREDIENTS

1/2 cup All Natural Peanut Butter
2 tbsps Soy Sauce Or Tamari (Gf)
2 tsps Ginger (grated)
1/8 tsp Sea Salt
1/2 cup Organic Coconut Milk
2 tbsps Lime Juice
1 tsp Sriracha Sauce (optional)
2 tsps Raw Honey

NUTRITION

AMOUNT PER SERVING

Calories	133	Fiber	1g
Fat	11g	Sugar	3g
Carbs	6g	Protein	4g

DIRECTIONS

01 Heat a small saucepan over low heat. Add all ingredients and stir until peanut butter is melted and everything is combined well.

02 Taste and season with additional salt, lime or chili.

03 Once prepared, keep refrigerated for up to 7 days.

NOTES

MAKE IT CRUNCHY
Use crunchy peanut butter or add 2 tbsp of chopped peanuts.
ADJUST SPICINESS
Use more or less Sriracha depending on your preference.
ADJUST CONSISTANCY
Add 1-2 tbsp of water if the sauce is too thick.
ADD FRESH HERBS
Add fresh cilantro or Thai basil.

Grilled Turkey Koftas

4 SERVINGS 20 MINUTES

INGREDIENTS

1 lb Extra Lean Ground Turkey (93% lean)
1/3 cup Quick Oats
1/4 Onion (grated)
2 cloves Garlic (crushed)
1/2 tsp Sea Salt
1/4 tsp Black Pepper
1/2 tsp Cumin
1/4 tsp Cinnamon
1 tsp Smoked Paprika (use regular if you don't have smoked)
3 tbsps Parsley (chopped)
1 Egg (lightly beaten)
3 tbsps Mint Leaves (chopped)
2 Tomato (sliced)
1/4 head Green Lettuce
1/2 cup Tzatziki
1 Red Onion (slices)
4 Whole Wheat Pita (With Pockets)

NUTRITION

AMOUNT PER SERVING

Calories	370	Fiber	4g
Fat	14g	Sugar	2g
Carbs	31g	Protein	30g

DIRECTIONS

01 Pre-heat oven to 400F.

02 In a large bowl, combine ground turkey, grated onion, garlic, egg, herbs and spices until well combined.

03 Form the mixture into 16 balls and wrap each around the tip of a skewer. Gently flatten out into an oval shape (the traditional kofta shape).

04 Place Koftas on a baking sheet and cook for 10 minutes. Turn koftas over and finish off by placing under the broil setting for 3-4 minutes.

05 Serve with Pita bread, sliced vegetables and tzatziki. Nutrition for 1 kofta skewer: Cal 49, Pro 6g, Carbs 1g, Fat 3g, Fiber 0g.

NOTES

STORAGE
Keep in the fridge for 4-5 days

VARIATIONS
Koftas can be made with ground beef, pork, lamb or chicken. Add additional spices such as chili, cayenne pepper or ground coriander for additional flavor.

NO EGGS
Mix 1 tbsp ground flax seed with 3 tbsp of warm water. Allow to sit for 5 minutes. Use in place of egg.

LOW CARB
Serve Koftas in lettuce wraps.

PAN FRY OR BBQ
Cook Koftas in a large skillet or on the BBQ grill.

Italian Turkey Stuffed Peppers

4 SERVINGS 30 MINUTES

INGREDIENTS

1 lb Extra Lean Ground Turkey
4 Red Bell Pepper
1 Onion (diced)
2 tsps Garlic (crushed)
1 tin Diced Tomatoes (14oz/498ml)
1 tsp Italian Seasoning
2 tsps Extra Virgin Olive Oil
1/2 tsp Sea Salt
1/4 tsp Red Pepper Flakes
1 1/2 cups Brown Rice (Cooked)
1/2 cup Basil Leaves (chopped)
1 cup Mozzarella Cheese (shredded)
2 tbsps Parmesan Cheese

NUTRITION

AMOUNT PER SERVING

Calories	409	Fiber	6g
Fat	19g	Sugar	7g
Carbs	35g	**Protein**	33g

DIRECTIONS

01 Preheat oven to 375F. Lightly coat a non-stick baking dish with a little olive oil or cooking spray.

02 Slice peppers in half from bottom to top, remove seeds and membrane. Arrange on the baking sheet.

03 Heat oil in a large skillet over medium high heat. Sauté garlic and onion for 1-2 minutes. Add ground turkey, Italian seasoning, salt and red pepper flakes. Cook for 4-5 minutes or until turkey is no longer pink. Drain any excess liquid.

04 Add diced tomatoes (including juice). Simmer for 2 minutes. Turn off heat and stir in rice, 1/2 of the mozzarella & parmesan cheese.

05 Divide the mixture between the prepared peppers. Sprinkle with remaining cheese.

06 Pour 1/2 cup water into the baking pan (this will help the peppers cook and become nice and soft). Bake uncovered for 30-35 minute or until peppers are tender. If the cheese begins to turn too brown, loosely cover with tin foil. Garnish with fresh basil.

NOTES

VEGETARIAN
Use Yves Ground Veggies round or substitute ground turkey for 1 can white beans and 1/2 cup crumbled tofu.

NO TURKEY
Use lean ground chicken, beef, pork or spicy Italian sausage.

NO BROWN RICE
Swap for cooked quinoa, farro, orzo or use cauliflower rice for a reduced carb option.

Mango Salsa Chicken Cups

4 SERVINGS 20 MINUTES

INGREDIENTS

- **1 lb** Chicken Thighs
- **1/4 tsp** Sea Salt & Black Pepper
- **1 tsp** Paprika
- **1/2 tsp** Onion Powder
- **2** Avocado (diced)
- **1 cup** Frozen Mango (defrosted and diced)
- **1/4 cup** Red Onion (finly diced)
- **1** Tomato (diced)
- **1/4 cup** Cucumber (finely chopped)
- **1** Lime (juice only)
- **1 pinch** Sea Salt (or more to taste)
- **1 head** Butter Lettuce

NUTRITION

AMOUNT PER SERVING

Calories	357	Fiber	10g
Fat	20g	Sugar	7g
Carbs	20g	Protein	27g

DIRECTIONS

01 Combine salt, pepper, paprika and onion powder. Season chicken on both sides.

02 Add 1 tbsp of coconut oil to a preheated, medium hot skillet. Cook chicken for 4-5 minutes per side or until cooked through. Cover and allow to sit for 2 minutes before slicing.

03 Combine avocado, tomato, mango, onion, cucumber and lime juice. Gently combine and season with salt as needed.

04 Arrange lettuce leaves on a large plate and divide the salsa between the leaves. Top with chicken and serve with fresh lime.

NOTES

MAKE IT SPICY
Add fresh sliced chili to the salsa mix.

STORAGE
Extra salsa can be kept refrigerated 2-3 days. Chicken can be kept for 4-5 days.

FEEDING KIDS
Let kids make their own lettuce wraps by placing individual ingredients in the middle of the table (sliced avocado, sliced chicken, mango pieces diced tomato etc).

ALTERNATIVE SERVING SUGGESTIONS
Serve with warm tortillas, rice or corn.

VEGETARAIN
Instead of chicken, combine a can rinsed black beans with the mango, avocado salsa. Season with extra salt, pepper and chili (if using).

FISH
Use grilled cod, halibut, snapper or other white fish for a light, summer twist.

Quick & Easy Chicken Tostadas

4 SERVINGS 20 MINUTES

INGREDIENTS

12 Tostada Shells
1 lb Chicken Breast (diced)
1 1/2 cups Salsa
1/2 cup Black Beans (rinsed)
1/2 cup Corn
2 Tomato (diced)
2 cups Green Lettuce (shredded)
4 ozs Cheddar Cheese (shredded)
1/2 cup Plain Greek Yogurt
1 Lime (optional)
1/4 cup Cilantro (optional)
1 tsp Hot Sauce (optional)

NUTRITION

AMOUNT PER SERVING

Calories	487	Fiber	9g
Fat	21g	Sugar	11g
Carbs	49g	Protein	26g

DIRECTIONS

01 Heat a large skillet over medium heat. Add 1 tsp cooking oil and sauté chicken for 5-6 minutes or until cooked through.

02 Add black beans, corn and 1/2 cup salsa. Cook for an additional 1-2 minutes

03 Place a small portion of the chicken mixture onto a tostada and top with diced tomatoes, shredded lettuce, cheese, Greek yogurt, lime, cilantro, hot sauce and salsa. Place another tostada on top and repeat process to create a 'stack' of 2-3 tostadas.

NOTES

PREP AHEAD
Bake or grill chicken on the weekend for a quick and easy weeknight meal.
NO CHICKEN
Use ground beef, pulled pork, veggie ground round, refried beans or cooked white fish.
MAKE IT MELTY
Add cheese to the final layer and place under the grill for 1-2 minutes until cheese melts (as shown in picture).
ADD EXTRA VEGGIES
Add a side salad or additional cut up veggie sticks.
FEEDING CHILDREN
Allow children to create their own 'stack'. Add additional ingredients such as grated carrots, avocado, diced cucumbers or peppers.

Sheet Pan Chicken Fajitas

4 SERVINGS 15 MINUTES

INGREDIENTS

1 lb Chicken Breast (sliced into tenders)
1 Red Bell Pepper (sliced)
1 Green Bell Pepper (sliced)
1 Orange Bell Pepper (sliced)
1 Red Onion (sliced)
1/2 Lime (juice)
1/4 cup Cilantro (chopped)
3/4 cup Basmati Rice
2 tbsps Taco Seasoning (recipe on page 81)
1 cup Guacamole
1/2 cup Plain Greek Yogurt

NUTRITION

AMOUNT PER SERVING

Calories	443	Fiber	7g
Fat	13g	Sugar	5g
Carbs	49g	Protein	34g

DIRECTIONS

01 Cook rice as directed on package.
02 Place chicken and vegetables into a large bowl, add lime juice, cilantro and taco seasoning. Gently toss to evenly coat chicken and vegetables.
03 Spread chicken and vegetables onto a large baking sheet.
04 Turn oven broil/grill setting to high.
05 Place baking sheet on the middle oven rack and cook for 10 minutes stirring 2-3 times to achieve even cooking and to prevent burning.
06 Divide rice, vegetables and chicken between bowls. Top with Greek yogurt, guacamole and serve with extra lime, cilantro, sriracha or salsa.

NOTES

NO OVEN BROIL/GRILL SETTING
Sauté vegetables and chicken in a large skillet or bake at 400F for 16-20 minutes.

STORAGE
Keep in the fridge for 4-5 days.

REDUCE CARBS
Use cauliflower rice or use lettuce as a wrap for the fajita mix.

ADDITIONAL SIDES
Serve with refried beans or a side of corn.

Prosciutto Wrapped Stuffed Chicken Breast

4 SERVINGS 25 MINUTES

INGREDIENTS

1 lb Chicken Breast
2 ozs Prosciutto
1/4 cup Goat Cheese
2 Red Bell Pepper (cut into large pieces)
2 Yellow Bell Pepper (cut into large pieces)
1 Zucchini (cut into large pieces)
1/2 Red Onion
4 cups Baby Spinach
2 cups Pasta Sauce (your favourite brand)
1 1/3 tbsps Extra Virgin Olive Oil
2 tbsps Pesto (Sundried Tomato or Basil)

NUTRITION

AMOUNT PER SERVING

Calories	417	Fiber	6g
Fat	16g	Sugar	12g
Carbs	25g	Protein	46g

DIRECTIONS

01 Preheat oven to 425F.

02 In a small bowl, mix together Goat's cheese and pesto.

03 In a large bowl combine vegetables and toss with olive oil and a pinch of salt and pepper.

04 Using a sharp paring knife, make a deep pocket (starting at the thickest side) into each chicken breast. Stuff with Goat's cheese, dividing evenly between each piece.

05 Cut the prosciutto in half, lengthways and wrap 2-3 pieces around each chicken breast. Wrapping as tight as you can without tearing the prosciutto.

06 Place chicken on one side of a baking sheet and spread the vegetables out on the other side. You may need to use 2 baking sheets depending on how many portions you are cooking.

07 Cook for 17-18 minutes or until juices run clear and internal temperature reaches 165F. Stir vegetables once during cooking.

08 Allow chicken to rest for 5 minutes covered in foil. Toss roasted vegetables with baby spinach and place in the oven to keep warm until ready to serve.

09 Heat pasta sauce and divide between plates. Slice chicken and place on top of pasta sauce, serve with warm vegetables.

NOTES

NO GOAT'S CHEESE
Use feta cheese, Swiss cheese or ricotta.

MEAL PREP
Chicken can be prepped 2-3 days ahead of time.

Taco Seasoning

10 SERVINGS 2 MINUTES

INGREDIENTS

1 tbsp Chili Powder
1 1/2 tsps Cumin
1/4 tsp Garlic Powder
1/4 tsp Onion Powder
1/4 tsp Dried Oregano
1/4 tsp Paprika
1 tsp Sea Salt
1 tsp Black Pepper
1/4 tsp Red Chili Flakes (option - add more or less to taste)

DIRECTIONS

01 Combine all ingredients until well mixed

NOTES

ADD CORNSTARCH
If using the seasoning to replicate a 'store bought' taco mix, add 1-2 tsp of cornstarch (which will help to create a thicker sauce).

NUTRITION

AMOUNT PER SERVING

Calories	5	Fiber	0g
Fat	0g	Sugar	0g
Carbs	1g	Protein	0g

Sheet Pan Turkey Meatloaf with Roasted Vegetable

4 SERVINGS 25 MINUTES

INGREDIENTS

1 lb Extra Lean Ground Turkey (93% lean)
1/3 cup Quick Oats
1/4 cup Onion (grated)
1/3 cup Ketchup
1 tbsp Yellow Mustard
1 Egg (lightly beaten)
2 tsps Worcestershire Sauce
1/2 tsp Sea Salt
1 tsp Marjoram
2 cups Green Beans
1/2 head Cauliflower
1 tbsp Olive Oil

NUTRITION

AMOUNT PER SERVING

Calories	302	Fiber		3g
Fat	15g	Sugar		8g
Carbs	18g	**Protein**		26g

DIRECTIONS

01 Preheat oven to 425F.

02 Combine ground turkey, oats, egg, grated onion, salt, marjoram, mustard and half the ketchup.

03 Mix half the ketchup and the Worcestershire sauce in a small container.

04 Divide the mixture and shape into 4 individual, freeform mini-meat loafs. Place on a baking sheet. Spoon the ketchup, Worcestershire mixture evenly over each meat loaf.

05 Toss vegetables with 1 tbsp of olive oil and spread on the baking sheet around the meatloaf.

06 Cook for 12 minutes. Remover and toss vegetables. Replace and cook for another 12 minutes (or until internal temperature reaches 165F.

NOTES

LIKE IS SPICY
Use 50/50 ketchup and BBQ sauce.
ADD MORE FLAVOUR
Use Dijon mustard instead of yellow mustard.
STORAGE
Keep in the fridge for 4-5 days.
FREEZER PREP
Follow steps 1-2. Place mixture in a large zip lock bag, store for up to 3 months.

Sheet Pan Pesto Chicken and Grilled Vegetables

4 SERVINGS 20 MINUTES

INGREDIENTS

1 lb Chicken Breast (slice horizontally to make 1" thick fillets)
1 tbsp Extra Virgin Olive Oil
1 tsp Garlic (crushed)
1 tsp Italian Seasoning
1 Red Bell Pepper (chopped)
1 Green Bell Pepper (chopped)
1 Zucchini (large, chopped)
1 cup Cherry Tomatoes
1 cup Red Onion (sliced)
1/4 cup Basil Pesto
6 cups Baby Spinach
1 cup Tzatziki (optional)

NUTRITION

AMOUNT PER SERVING

Calories	374	Fiber	4g
Fat	17g	Sugar	8g
Carbs	17g	Protein	40g

DIRECTIONS

01 Turn on broil/grill setting of oven.

02 In a large bowl, gently toss chopped vegetables with olive oil, garlic and Italian seasoning.

03 Place chicken onto a large baking sheet, divide pesto between chicken and spread over top. Arrange vegetables around chicken.

04 Place on the middle rack underneath the grill. Cook for 10 minutes, stirring vegetables occasionally to prevent burning.

05 Divide baby spinach between plates and top with grilled chicken and vegetables. Serve with tzatziki and fresh lemon.

NOTES

ADDITIONAL SERVING OPTIONS
Rice, potatoes, pita bread or pasta. These items have not been factored into the nutrition breakdown.

ADD FETA
Once chicken and vegetables are cooked, add crumbled feta.

KEEP IT SIMPLE
Stick with 2 vegetables (such as red peppers & zucchini) or buy pre-cut vegetables.

STORAGE
Keep in the fridge for up to 5 days.

Pasta & Stir Fry

Creamy Pea Pesto & Bacon Pasta

Garlic Shrimp & Baby Spinach Pasta

Creamy Tomato Chicken with Green Vegetables

Creamy Sundried Tomato & Mushroom Pasta

Skillet Chicken Bruschetta Pasta

Pesto Gnocchi Skillet with Broccoli & Sausage

Weeknight Spaghetti Bolognese

Chicken Satay Stir Fry

Honey Garlic Shrimp Stir Fry

Soy & Ginger Beef Stir Fry

Teriyaki Meatballs & Stir Fry Vegetables

Creamy Pea Pesto and Bacon Pasta

4 SERVINGS 30 MINUTES

INGREDIENTS

4 cups Frozen Peas
1 cup Plain Yogurt
2 Egg (beaten)
1/4 cup Pesto
3 tbsps Lemon Juice
6 ozs Penne Pasta (or gluten free pasta)
8 slices Bacon (nitrate fee)
1 pinch Sea Salt & Black Pepper (to taste)
2 tbsps Parmesan Cheese

NUTRITION

AMOUNT PER SERVING

Calories	520	Fiber	14g
Fat	20g	Sugar	17g
Carbs	54g	**Protein**	34g

DIRECTIONS

01 Bring a large pot of water to a boil. Dunk peas in boiling water for 60 seconds. Drain peas and keep the water for cooking the pasta.

02 Cook bacon in a large skillet. Remove and place on paper towel to absorb excess fat. Allow to cool, chop into small pieces.

03 Add peas, pesto, parmesan and lemon juice to a food processor or blender. Puree until just combined (leaving some of the peas whole).

04 In a small bowl, mix together eggs and yogurt.

05 Cook pasta as directed on packet.

06 Drain pasta, reserving 1 cup of cooking water and return pasta to the pot. Turn heat down to the lowest setting.

07 Add the pea pesto mix to pasta, gently stir. Pour in yogurt egg mix and stir over low heat for 1 minute. Remove from heat. Add a small splash of reserved pasta water if the sauce is too thick.

08 Stir through bacon pieces, season with salt and pepper if needed.

NOTES

VEGETARIAN
Replace bacon with tempeh or try coconut bacon.

NO BACON
Replace bacon with grilled chicken or shrimp.

REDUCE CARBS
Replace 1/2 the pasta with zucchini ribbons. Use a vegetable peeler to create thin strips. Add the zucchini to the pasta water for 1 minute to quickly cook before serving.

ADD SOME HEAT
Add 1 tsp red chili flakes or sriracha sauce.

Garlic Shrimp and Baby Spinach Pasta

4 SERVINGS 20 MINUTES

INGREDIENTS

- **8 ozs** Whole Grain Spaghetti (or gluten free)
- **1 lb** Shrimp (peeled and deveined)
- **8 cups** Baby Spinach (fresh)
- **2 cups** Cherry Tomatoes (cut in half)
- **1 tsp** Chili Flakes (optional)
- **6 cloves** Garlic (crushed)
- **1** Lemon (juice)
- **1/4 cup** Butter
- **1 cup** Vegetable Broth
- **2 Pinch** Salt And Pepper (to taste)
- **1/4 cup** Parsley (fresh, chopped)
- **1/4 cup** Heavy Cream

NUTRITION

AMOUNT PER SERVING

Calories	490	Fiber	7g
Fat	20g	Sugar	5g
Carbs	47g	Protein	37g

DIRECTIONS

01 Bring a large pot of water to the boil and cook pasta until al dente (according to package directions).

02 Melt butter in a large skillet over medium-high heat, add 2 tsp crushed garlic and chili, sauté for 1-2 minutes.

03 Add shrimp and continue to sauté, stirring frequently until shrimp are pink on the outside and white in the middle, 3-4 minutes. Just before shrimp is cooked, add tomatoes, spinach, lemon juice and season with salt and pepper. Sauté for 1 minute until spinach has turned bright green and just begins to wilt. Place shrimp and spinach mix into a bowl and cover.

04 Use the same pan the prawns were cooked in. Add vegetable broth and 1 tsp crushed garlic. Bring to a boil, scraping down any garlic that has stuck to the bottom of the pan. Add cream, simmer for 2-3 minutes until the broth has reduced by half.

05 Add the shrimp, spinach and cooked pasta back to the pan. Toss to combine.

06 Garnish with fresh parsley and some lemon zest.

NOTES

NO SHRIMP
Substitute with chicken or scallops.

REDUCE CARBOHYDRATES
Use half the amount of pasta and replace with zucchini ribbons. To make zucchini ribbons, use a vegetable peeler to create long strips. Add the zucchini ribbons to the pan after step 3 and allow to cook for 1-2 minutes to soften.

REDUCE FAT
Replace the heavy cream with equal amounts for Greek yogurt.
This will reduce the fat by approximately 5g/serve.

Creamy Tomato Chicken with Green Vegetables

4 SERVINGS 20 MINUTES

INGREDIENTS

1 lb Chicken Breast (sliced)
1 White Onion (diced)
2 cloves Garlic (crushed)
1 Zucchini (sliced)
2 cups Broccoli (cut into florets)
3 cups Pasta Sauce
1/4 cup Heavy Cream
1 tbsp Extra Virgin Olive Oil

NUTRITION

AMOUNT PER SERVING

Calories	391	Fiber	7g
Fat	15g	Sugar	14g
Carbs	25g	Protein	41g

DIRECTIONS

01 Heat oil in a large skillet, add onion and garlic sauté for 2-3 minutes. Add sliced chicken and continue to cook for 2-3 minutes (chicken will finish cooking with vegetables). Add zucchini and broccoli and continue to cook until chicken is cooked through.

02 Add pasta sauce and cream. Bring to a boil then reduce heat to a simmer. Cover and cook until broccoli and zucchini is tender.

NOTES

SERVE WITH
Serve with your favorite pasta, veggie spirals (fresh or from frozen) or on a bed of baby spinach. Garnish with fresh basil and parmesan cheese.

STORAGE
Store in the fridge for 4-5 days or in the freezer for up to 3 months.

PASTA SAUCE
Use your favorite store bought pasta sauce.

Creamy Chicken, Mushroom with Sundried Tomatoes

4 SERVINGS 30 MINUTES

INGREDIENTS

- **1 lb** Chicken Thighs (cut into 1" strips)
- **2 cups** Penne Pasta (uncooked measure)
- **1** Onion (diced)
- **3** Garlic (cloves, crushed)
- **8 ozs** Mushrooms (sliced, approximately 3 cups)
- **2 cups** Baby Spinach
- **2 tbsps** Sun Dried Tomatoes (sliced)
- **1/2 cup** White Cooking Wine
- **1 cup** Chicken Stock
- **1/2 cup** Milk (full fat, or use your favourite plant based milk)
- **1/2 cup** Parmesan Cheese (Fresh, grated)
- **1 tsp** Lemon Zest (approx' 1/2 lemon)
- **2 tbsps** Corn Starch
- **1/4 cup** Basil Leaves (optional, for serving)
- **2 tsps** Extra Virgin Olive Oil

NUTRITION

AMOUNT PER SERVING

Calories	452	Fiber	3g
Fat	13g	Sugar	6g
Carbs	45g	Protein	36g

DIRECTIONS

01 Cook pasta as directed on packet. Drain and set aside until ready to use.

02 Heat a large skillet over medium-high heat. Add olive oil and sauté chicken for 4-5 minutes or until nicely browned and cooked through. Remove chicken from skillet and cover.

03 Using the same skillet, add remaining olive oil, garlic, onion and mushrooms. Sauté for 3-4 minutes, scraping any crunchy bits off the bottom.

04 Add wine and stock and bring to a boil, reduce heat and simmer for 5 minutes or until liquid has reduced by approximately 25%. Add spinach, stirring for 1-2 minutes until bright green and wilted.

05 Add half the milk, grated parmesan cheese and cooked chicken back to the skillet. Stir until combined.

06 Combine corn starch with remaining milk, mix until smooth. Slowly pour corn starch mix into the skillet, stir until well combined. Add pasta and simmer for 2-3 minutes or until sauce thickens. Finish by stirring through lemon zest. Season with salt and pepper if needed.

07 Serve and garnish with fresh basil leaves and additional parmesan.

NOTES

VEGETARIAN
Add 1 cup cooked green peas (add in at step 5), and 1 sliced zucchini (sauté alongside mushrooms).

NO WINE
Replace wine with chicken or vegetable broth.

GLUTEN FREE
Use gluten free pasta (my favorite brand is Catelli).

Skillet Chicken Bruschetta Pasta

4 SERVINGS 20 MINUTES

INGREDIENTS

- **1 lb** Chicken Breast
- **2 cups** Fusilli Pasta (uncooked measure)
- **4** Tomato (diced)
- **4 cloves** Garlic (crushed)
- **1/4 cup** Basil Pesto
- **2 tbsps** Balsamic Vinegar
- **1/2 cup** Basil Leaves
- **1/4 cup** Parmigiano Reggiano
- **1/2 cup** Red Onion (finely diced)
- **2 tbsps** Balsamic Reduction (Optional)

DIRECTIONS

01 In a large bowl, combine diced tomatoes, garlic, pesto, onion, balsamic vinegar and a pinch of salt and pepper. Can be prepped up to 24 hours ahead.

02 Cook pasta as directed on packet. Do not over cook as it will continue to absorb some of the juices from the tomatoes.

03 Season chicken breast with salt and pepper. Heat olive oil in a large skillet and cook chicken for 3-4 minutes per side or until just cooked. Remove from pan cover and allow to rest for 2-3 minutes.

04 Add cooked pasta and tomato mixture to the same skillet the chicken was cooked in. Warm over medium heat for 2-3 minutes.

05 Slice chicken and add to pasta, gently toss until evenly combined.

06 Remove from heat and divide between bowls. Serve with fresh Parmesan cheese, a drizzle of Balsamic reduction and fresh basil.

NOTES

MEAL PREP OR TIME SAVER
Bake or grill chicken ahead of time or use rotisserie chicken.

ADD-IN'S
For extra flavor, add any of the following: sliced prosciutto, crumbled feta cheese, olives or red chili flakes.

VEGETARIAN
Instead of chicken use 1 x 14oz can of cannellini beans. Add extra salt, pepper and pesto for additional flavor. Consider using whole grain wheat, spelt or kamut pasta to boost protein.

GLUTEN FREE
Use gluten free pasta (my favorite brand is Catelli).

Pesto Gnocchi Skillet with Sausage and Broccolini

4 SERVINGS 20 MINUTES

INGREDIENTS

1 lbs Sweet Italian Turkey Sausages (casings removed)
1 lbs Gnocchi (fresh or frozen)
2 cloves Garlic (crushed)
1 lbs Broccolini
1/4 cup Pesto
1/4 cup Parmigiano Reggiano (fresh, grated)
1 tsp Black Pepper

NUTRITION

AMOUNT PER SERVING

Calories	482	**Fiber**	6g
Fat	17g	**Sugar**	1g
Carbs	48g	**Protein**	30g

DIRECTIONS

01 Chop broccolini into 2-3" pieces.

02 Bring a large pot of water to the boil. Cook gnocchi as directed. Use a slotted spoon and remove the gnocchi once they float to the surface. Skip this step if using 'skillet' gnocchi - which is already pre-cooked.

03 Add the broccolini to the boiling water (after removing gnocchi). Cook for 2-3 minutes until bright green but still a little crunchy. Remove from water. Reserve one cup of the cooking water.

04 In a large skillet, add sausage links (casings removed) and cook over medium heat. Use a wooden spoon to break the sausage into small pieces. Add a little cooking water if the sausage begins to stick. Add garlic.

05 Add broccolini, gnocchi and pesto, continue to cook for 2-3 minutes. Add additional water if needed.

06 Add grated Parmigiano Reggiano. And stir until just combined. Divide between plates.

NOTES

NO TURKEY SAUSAGE
Use chicken, beef or pork sausage. Choose sweet, mild or hot depending on your preference.

NO BROCCOLINI
Use broccoli or asparagus instead.

VEGETARIAN
Use Yves ground round or your favorite brand of plant based sausage.

EXTRA VEGETABLES
Add fresh diced tomatoes or diced red peppers for additional flavor.

GLUTEN FREE
You can find gluten free gnocchi in many grocery stores. Just make sure you check labels to ensure it is gluten free.

Weeknight Spaghetti Bolognese

4 SERVINGS 20 MINUTES

INGREDIENTS

1 lb Extra Lean Ground Beef
1 Yellow Onion (diced)
1 tbsp Garlic (crushed)
2 Carrot (diced)
1 stalk Celery (diced)
4 cups Baby Spinach (shredded)
1 tin Crushed Tomatoes (28oz/796ml)
1/4 cup Pesto
2 tbsps Tomato Paste
1 tsp Oregano (dried)
1/2 tsp Sea Salt & Black Pepper (more or less to season)
1/4 tsp Red Chili Flakes (optional)
6 ozs Spaghetti (or gluten free pasta)

NUTRITION

AMOUNT PER SERVING

Calories	457	**Fiber**	5g
Fat	18g	**Sugar**	7g
Carbs	41g	**Protein**	31g

DIRECTIONS

01 Sauté onions and garlic for 2-3 minutes. Add carrots and celery. Cook for another 2-3 minutes or until they begin to soften.

02 Add ground beef and cook until evenly browned, breaking up and pieces as you cook.

03 Add crushed tomato, tomato paste, dried oregano, red chili flakes and pesto. Bring to a boil and then reduce to a simmer. Simmer for 15 minutes. Stir through chopped spinach and continue to simmer until spinach has wilted. Season with salt and pepper as needed.

04 While sauce is simmering, cook spaghetti as directed on packet.

NOTES

LOWER CARBS
Serve with veggie noodles (spiralized zucchini or squash).

FEEDING KIDS
If you have kids who don't like 'chunky bits', place the tomato/vegetable sauce (BEFORE you add the meat) in a blender and puree for 20-30 seconds. Brown the meat and then pour the sauce over top - simmer for 15 minutes.

STORAGE
Refrigerate for 4-5 days or freeze for up to 3 months.

VEGETARIAN
Use veggie ground round or lentils instead of meat.

BIG BATCH COOKING
Bolognese sauce is perfect for 'big batch cooking'. Make 2-3x the recipe. Allow the sauce to cook and place in freezer safe containers.

Chicken Satay Stir Fry

4 SERVINGS 25 MINUTES

INGREDIENTS

1 lb Chicken Breast
1 cup Broccoli (cut into small florets)
1 cup Snap Peas
1 Red Bell Pepper (thinly sliced)
2 Carrot (thinly sliced)
1 cup Red Onion (thinly sliced)
4 cups Purple Cabbage (shredded)
1/3 cup Soy Sauce Or Tamari (Gf)
2 tsps Sriracha Sauce (or other hot sauce)
2 tbsps Ginger (fresh, grated)
2 tbsps Honey
1 1/3 tbsps Garlic (crushed)
1/3 cup Peanut Butter
2 tsps Coconut Oil
1/2 cup Chicken Broth
1 tbsp Corn Starch

NUTRITION

AMOUNT PER SERVING

Calories	474	Fiber	7g
Fat	19g	Sugar	20g
Carbs	37g	**Protein**	46g

DIRECTIONS

01 Cut chicken horizontally so each piece is 1/2" thick.

02 In a small bowl combine 1tbsp. soy sauce, 1 tbsp. peanut butter, 1 tsp garlic, 1 tsp ginger and 2 tsp oil. Add chicken breast and coat with marinade (can be done 48 hours ahead of time).

03 In a separate bowl combine vegetable broth, remaining soy sauce, honey, sriracha sauce, grated ginger, peanut butter and corn starch. Mix until well combined. Set aside.

04 Turn oven to broil/grill and arrange the rack to the second highest position.

05 Place chicken on a baking tray lined with tin foil. Place under the grill and cook for 7-10 minutes.

06 While chicken is cooking, heat coconut oil in a wok or large pan over medium-high heat. Add garlic and onion and cook for 1-2 minutes. Add remaining vegetables and continuously stir with two wooden spatulas (using the same motion as if you were tossing a salad). Cook for 5-7 minutes or until the vegetables just begin to soften and the broccoli is bright green.

07 Add stir-fry sauce and cook for 1-2 minutes letting the sauce thicken slightly.

08 Slice the chicken into long strips and serve over stir-fry vegetables. Garnish with peanuts.

NOTES

SAVE TIME
Save time in the kitchen by purchasing 1 bag of pre-cut stir-fry vegetable mix and 1 bag of coleslaw mix instead of buying and chopping all the vegetables individually.

KID FRIENDLY COOKING
Marinade chicken with soy sauce, peanut butter and honey. Remove a 'kid portion' of vegetables before you add the sauce, add a small amount of soy sauce, honey, peanut butter to the 'kids veggies'. Serve over rice.

SERVING SUGGESTIONS
Serve with rice or noodles or simply serve as is for a grain free option.

Honey Garlic Shrimp Stir Fry

4 SERVINGS 20 MINUTES

INGREDIENTS

1 lb Shrimp (peeled, devined)
1 cup Snow Peas
1 Red Bell Pepper (sliced)
1 Carrot (shredded into ribbons)
1 cup Broccoli (cut into small florrets)
2 tbsps Soy Sauce Or Tamari (Gf)
2 tbsps Peanut Butter
1 tsp Ginger (grated)
1 tbsp Honey
1 tsp Garlic (crushed)
1/2 cup Vegetable Stock (broth)
2 tsps Corn Starch
1/4 cup Cilantro (chopped, optional)
1 cup Vermicelli Rice Noodles (cooked as directed on packet)

NUTRITION

AMOUNT PER SERVING

Calories	314	Fiber		4g
Fat		6g	Sugar	8g
Carbs		38g	**Protein**	30g

DIRECTIONS

01 Combine soy sauce, vegetable broth, peanut butter, honey, ginger, garlic, cilantro and corn starch. Whisk until well combined.

02 Chop all vegetables.

03 Pre-heat a large wok or skillet to medium-high heat. Add 1 tbsp of avocado or coconut oil. Add shrimp and cook for 4-5 minutes or until shrimp have just turned pink and 80% cooked through (they will finish cooking with the vegetables).

04 Remove shrimp, add vegetables to the same wok and cook for 5-6 minutes on medium-high heat or until vegetables just begin to soften.

05 Add shrimp back to the wok and pour over sauce mix. Cook for an additional 2-3 minutes or until sauce slightly thickens.

06 Stir through cooked rice noodles and serve. Garnish with extra cilantro or wedges of lime.

NOTES

NO NOODLES
Serve over cooked rice.
EXTRA VEGETABLES
Use any combination of vegetables.
NO SHRIMP
Use tofu or chicken instead.

Soy & Ginger Beef Stir Fry

4 SERVINGS 25 MINUTES

INGREDIENTS

- **8 ozs** Top Sirloin Steak (thinly sliced)
- **1 cup** Broccoli (cut into small florets)
- **1** Red Bell Pepper (thinly sliced)
- **2 cups** Coleslaw Mix
- **1** Zucchini (small, sliced)
- **2 tsps** Ginger (grated)
- **1 tbsp** Raw Honey
- **2 cloves** Garlic (crushed)
- **1/4 cup** Soy Sauce Or Tamari (Gf)
- **1/4 cup** All Natural Peanut Butter
- **1/4 cup** Beef Broth
- **1 tsp** Hot Sauce (optional)
- **1/2 cup** Cashews (optional)
- **2 ozs** Rice Stick Noodles

NUTRITION

AMOUNT PER SERVING

Calories	433	Fiber	4g
Fat	25g	Sugar	11g
Carbs	35g	**Protein**	22g

DIRECTIONS

01 In a zip lock bag (or other container) combine beef with half the ginger, garlic and soy sauce. Can be done up to 2 day ahead.

02 Cook rice noodles as directed on packet.

03 Preheat a large skillet or wok to medium-high heat. Add 1 tbsp oil and cook beef for 2-3 minutes, or until 'just' done. Remove beef, cover and set aside.

04 In the same pan add the broccoli, peppers and zucchini. Sauté for 2-3 minutes until vegetables begin to soften. Add coleslaw mix and cook for another 2-3 minutes.

05 Add rice noodles and beef to the vegetables. Add the remaining ginger, garlic, soy sauce, honey, peanut butter and broth. Turn heat down and cook for 2-3 minutes or until sauce has slightly thickened.

06 Divide between bowls and serve with cashews.

NOTES

NO NOODLES
Serve over rice.

REDUCE CARBS
Leave out the rice noodles and add an extra 1-2 cups of shredded cabbage or other vegetables.

NO BEEF
Use chicken, shrimp, pork, tofu or tempeh.

EXTRA FLAVOUR
Serve with fresh lime, cilantro and hot sauce.

Teriyaki Meatballs & Stir-fry Vegetables

4 SERVINGS 40 MINUTES

INGREDIENTS

- **1 lb** Extra Lean Ground Turkey
- **1** Egg (lightly beaten)
- **1/4 cup** Dried Bread Crumbs (or gluten free)
- **2 tbsps** Cilantro (finely chopped)
- **1/2 tsp** Sea Salt & Black Pepper (each)
- **1 tsp** Garlic (crushed)
- **2 cups** Snap Peas
- **1** Carrot (cut into thin strips)
- **3/4 cup** Basmati Rice
- **1/2 cup** Teriyaki Sauce (recipe on page 99)
- **2 stalks** Green Onion
- **2 tbsps** Sesame Seeds (optional)

NUTRITION

AMOUNT PER SERVING

Calories	431	Fiber	4g
Fat	13g	Sugar	8g
Carbs	47g	Protein	31g

DIRECTIONS

01 Cook rice as directed on packet.

02 In a large bowl, combine ground turkey, egg, bread crumbs, chopped cilantro, salt & pepper and garlic. Gently mix together with a fork or your hands. Form into small meatballs.

03 Heat a large skillet over medium-high heat. Add 1/4 cup water. When the water is boiling, add snap peas and carrots. Cook for 2-3 minutes or until beginning to soften (add additional water if needed). Remove from skillet and set aside.

04 Pour out any excess water. Add 1 tbsp cooking oil to the skillet and add the meatballs. Cook for 2-3 minutes until golden brown on the bottom and then turn, repeating until all sides are golden brown.

05 Add vegetables back to the skillet, pour over teriyaki sauce. Stir gently until combined. Simmer for 5-7 minutes.

06 Serve over steamed rice. Garnish with green onion, sesame seeds or additional cilantro.

NOTES

SAVE TIME

Use pre-made or frozen meatballs. Buy pre-made Teriyaki sauce.

MEAL PREP

Meat balls can be prepped 3-4 days ahead of time. Prep a double batch and freeze half the meat balls (raw) for another meal.

SERVING SIZE

One serving equals approximately 5 to 6 meatballs.

NO TURKEY

Substitute turkey with ground pork, beef or chicken.

Teriyaki Sauce

4 SERVINGS 5 MINUTES

INGREDIENTS

- **1/2 cup** Water (plus 2 extra TBSP)
- **3 tbsps** Soy Sauce Or Tamari (Gf)
- **2 tbsps** Mirin Sauce (find it in the soy sauce aisle)
- **2 tsps** Ginger (fresh, grated)
- **1 tsp** Garlic (crushed)
- **2 tbsps** Honey
- **1 tbsp** Cornstarch

NUTRITION

AMOUNT PER SERVING

Calories	69	Fiber	0g
Fat	0g	Sugar	11g
Carbs	16g	Protein	1g

DIRECTIONS

01 In a small pot, combine all ingredients (except cornstarch and extra 2 TBSP water). Bring to a simmer.

02 Combine cornstarch and additional water, mix together to form a slurry. Pour into sauce mixture and stir well, continue to simmer until sauce thickens.

03 Use as a stir-fry sauce, add to grilled chicken or fish or pour over meatballs.

NOTES

MIRIN

Mirin is a sweet Japanese rice wine, you can usually find it in the soy sauce aisle of the grocery store. If you can't find mirin you can substitute dry white wine or rice vinegar mixed with 1 tsp sugar.

Beef & Pork

Camping Chili

Classic Shepherd's Pie

Grilled Lemon Garlic Steak Skewers

Muffin Tin Mini Meatloaf

Satay Beef Skewers

Skinny Beef Stroganoff

Dry Rub Pulled Pork

Pulled Pork Lettuce Cups

Sausage, Apple & Sauteed Cabbage

Sweet Balsamic Pork Tenderloin

Camping Chili

6 SERVINGS 45 MINUTES

INGREDIENTS

1 lb Extra Lean Ground Beef
1 tin Red Kidney Beans (19oz/570ml, drained and rinsed)
1 tin Refried Beans (14oz/398ml)
1 tin Diced Tomatoes (28oz/796ml, keep the juice)
1 Yellow Onion (diced)
1 Carrot (diced)
2 stalks Celery (diced)
1 Red Bell Pepper (diced)
1 Green Bell Pepper (diced)
2 cloves Garlic (crushed)
1/2 cup Beef Broth
2 tbsps Chili Powder
2 tsps Cumin
1/4 tsp Dried Oregano
1 Pinch Salt And Pepper (to taste)
1/4 cup Cilantro (fresh, chopped - optional)

DIRECTIONS

1. Heat oil in a large saucepan, sauté onion and garlic for 1-2 minutes. Add ground beef, cook for 5-7 minutes or until meat is cooked through and no longer pink.
2. Add carrots, celery, red & green peppers and dry spices, continue to cook for another 3-4 minutes.
3. Add beans, canned tomatoes and broth. Bring to a boil and then reduce heat to a simmer for 20-25 minutes.

NOTES

ERVE WITH
Rice, corn chips or a whole grain roll (not included in nutrition breakdown).

AVE TIME
Use a packet of Chili season mix instead of the dry herbs and spices.

LOW COOKER
Brown beef with onion and garlic for 4-5 minutes. Add to the slow cooker with all other ingredients. Cook on high for 2-3 hours or low for 5-6 hours.

TORAGE
Refrigerate for 4-5 days or store in the freezer for up to 3 months.

EGETARIAN
Instead of beef use an additional 2 cup of beans or lentils. Alternatively, use a prepared, plant based product such as Yves Veggie Ground.

NUTRITION
AMOUNT PER SERVING

Calories	276	Fiber	13g
Fat	8g	Sugar	8g
Carbs	34g	Protein	26g

Classic Shepherd's Pie

4 SERVINGS 1 HOUR

INGREDIENTS

- **1 lb** Extra Lean Ground Beef
- **1** Onion (diced)
- **2** Garlic, Cloves (crushed)
- **1 stalk** Celery (chopped)
- **1** Carrot (diced)
- **1/2 cup** Frozen Peas
- **1/2 cup** Frozen Corn
- **1/2 cup** Beef Broth
- **1/2 tsp** Sea Salt
- **2 tbsps** Ketchup
- **2 tbsps** Worcestershire Sauce
- **1 tbsp** Yellow Mustard
- **1 tbsp** Corn Flour
- **1 tsp** Dried Thyme
- **1/2 tsp** Dried Rosemary
- **2 lbs** Russet Potato (scrubbed and cubed)
- **1/4 cup** Milk Of Choice
- **1/4 cup** Parmesan Cheese
- **1 tbsp** Olive Oil

NUTRITION

AMOUNT PER SERVING

Calories	411	Fiber	4g
Fat	18g	Sugar	6g
Carbs	33g	Protein	28g

DIRECTIONS

01 Preheat oven to 375F.

02 Steam potatoes until soft (approximately 10-12 minutes). Add 2 tbsp of Parmesan cheese, milk and 1 tbsp butter, mash until smooth. Season with salt and pepper. If the mash is too dry add 1 tbsp of milk at a time until you reach desired consistency.

03 Heat oil in a large skillet over medium high heat. Add onion, garlic, carrots and celery. Saute for 2-3 minutes. Add ground beef and continue to cook for another 5-6 minutes or until beef is completely cooked.

04 Mix corn starch with a small amount of broth to form a slurry, set aside. Add remaining beef broth, frozen vegetables, ketchup, Worcestershire sauce, dried herbs and sea salt. Pour in corn starch mix. Bring to a boil and then reduce heat to a simmer for 5.

05 Transfer mixture to a large oven safe dish. Gently spread the mashed potato over top. Use a fork to scrape the top of the potatoes to make ridges. Sprinkle remaining Parmesan cheese on top.

06 Bake for 35 minutes or until potatoes turn golden. Remove from oven and let cool for 10 minutes before serving.

NOTES

NO BEEF
Use ground turkey, swap the beef broth to chicken broth.

EXTRA FLAVOUR
Add 1 tsp horseradish and 1/4 tsp cayenne pepper.

MAKE IT CHEESY
Add 1/2 cup of grated cheddar to the mashed potato.

Grilled Lemon Garlic Steak Skewers

4 SERVINGS 20 MINUTES

INGREDIENTS

- **1 lb** Sirloin Steak (cut into 1"cubes)
- **2 tbsps** Extra Virgin Olive Oil
- **4** Garlic cloves (crushed)
- **2 tbsps** Lemon Juice
- **1 tsp** Italian Seasoning
- **1** Red Bell Pepper (cut into wedges)
- **1** Orange Bell Pepper (cut into wedges)
- **2** Zucchini (Sliced length way into 1/4" strips)
- **1 cup** Cherry Tomatoes
- **1/2** Red Onion (cut into rounds -keep together)
- **1 cup** Tzatziki

NUTRITION

AMOUNT PER SERVING

Calories	322	Fiber	3g
Fat	17g	Sugar	7g
Carbs	15g	Protein	29g

DIRECTIONS

01 Preheat BBQ or grill to medium heat. *see notes for oven directions.

02 Divide olive oil, crushed garlic, lemon juice and dried Italian herbs between 2 bowls. Place steak in one bowl and coat evenly - this can be done 2-3 days ahead of time. Place vegetables in the other bowl, toss with oil and seasoning.

03 Thread steak onto skewers separating each piece with a cherry tomato.

04 Place skewers and vegetables onto the preheated grill. Turn steak every 2 minute so each side cooks evenly (allow to rest while vegetables continue to cook). Turn vegetables once during cooking - approximately 10-12 minutes.

05 Divide skewers and vegetables between plates and serve with Tzatziki.

NOTES

PREP AHEAD

Steak and vegetables can be prepped up to 2-3 days ahead of cooking.

ADDITIONAL SIDE

Slice mini potatoes in half, drizzle with a small amount of olive oil (1 tsp/person), place on the grill and cook with the skewers and vegetables.

ADD FETA

Once the vegetables are cooked, add crumbled feta.

KEEP IT SIMPLE

Stick with 2 vegetables such as red peppers & zucchini.

NO OUT-DOOR GRILL/BBQ

Set the broil setting in the oven to high and move the cooking rack to the middle of the oven. Arrange skewers and vegetables on a large baking tray and cook for 3-4 minutes per side, flip vegetables 3-4 times to prevent burning.

Mini Muffin Tin Meatloaf

4 SERVINGS 30 MINUTES

INGREDIENTS

1 lb Extra Lean Ground Beef (93% lean)
1/3 cup Quick Oats
1/4 cup Onion (grated)
1/3 cup Ketchup
1 tbsp Yellow Mustard
1 Egg (lightly beaten)
2 tsps Worcestershire Sauce
1/2 tsp Sea Salt
1 tsp Italian Seasoning
4 smalls Yellow Potato (approximately 1.5 lbs)
2 Carrot
1 tbsp Butter
1/4 cup Milk (of choice)
1/2 cup Cheddar Cheese (grated)

NUTRITION

AMOUNT PER SERVING

Calories	344	Fiber	2g
Fat	16g	Sugar	9g
Carbs	22g	Protein	27g

DIRECTIONS

01 Preheat oven to 400F.

02 Lightly grease a 12-hole muffin tray.

03 Scrub potatoes and cut into 2" pieces. Scrub the carrot and slice into rounds. Place carrots and potatoes in a large pot and add just enough water to cover the vegetables. Bring to a boil and cook for 8-10 minutes or until soft. Drain vegetables, add butter and milk and mash until smooth. Stir through grated cheese.

04 Combine ground beef, oats, egg, grated onion, salt, Italian seasoning, mustard and half the ketchup. Mix until just combined.

05 Mix the remaining ketchup and Worcestershire sauce in a small container.

06 Divide the mixture between the muffin tin and gently press the mixture down to fill the hole approximately 1/2 full. Add a spoonful of the ketchup, Worcestershire mixture to each mini meatloaf.

07 Top each mini meat loaf with a scoop of the mashed sweet potato/carrot combo. Use an ice-cream scoop for a perfect 'muffin' shape.

08 Bake for 20-25 minutes.

NOTES

SERVE WITH
Steamed, roasted or raw vegetables or a large mixed salad.
LIKE IS SPICY
Use 50/50 ketchup and BBQ sauce.
ADD MORE FLAVOUR
Use Dijon mustard instead of yellow mustard.

Satay Beef Skewers

4 SERVINGS 20 MINUTES

INGREDIENTS

1 lb Top Sirloin Steak (trimmed of fat)
1 tsp Ginger (fresh, grated)
1 tsp Garlic (crushed)
1/2 tsp Onion Powder
2 tbsps Soy Sauce Or Tamari (Gf)
1 tbsp Avocado Oil (or other high heat cooking oil)
1/2 tsp Cumin
2 tbsps Sweet Chili Sauce
1/2 tsp Turmeric

NUTRITION

AMOUNT PER SERVING

Calories	298	Fiber	0g
Fat	12g	Sugar	4g
Carbs	5g	Protein	24g

DIRECTIONS

01 Slice steak into strips approximately 2-3" long and 1/8" thick.

02 Combine all other ingredients and whisk into a smooth marinade.

03 Divide meat and thread onto skewers (2 skewers per person, or 1 large skewer each).

04 Place Skewers in a large ziplock bag and pour over marinade. Gently massage the marinade into the skewers to evenly coat the meat. Seal the bag and allow to marinate in the fridge for at least 2 hours.

05 Remove skewers from marinade and place on a preheated grill. Cook for 1-2 minutes. Flip over and cook for another 2 minutes or until nicely browned, flip back to the first side and cook for another 1-2 minutes - or until your steak is cooked to your liking. Transfer to a plate and cover with foil, allow to rest for 2 minutes before serving.

NOTES

SERVE WITH

Loaded Fried Rice & Spicy Satay Sauce

ADDITIONAL FLAVOUR

Add 1 tsp fish sauce and 1 stalk of fresh lemon grass. Bruise the lemon grass by hitting with the back of a large chef's knife then mince and add to marinade.

ADD SOME HEAT

Add 1/8 tsp cayenne pepper or diced red chilli to the marinade.

Skinny Beef Stroganoff

6 SERVINGS 4 HOURS

INGREDIENTS

1 1/2 lbs Sirloin Steak (cut into 1/2" strips)
1 lb Cremini Mushrooms (sliced)
1 Zucchini (sliced into ribbons)
1 White Onion (sliced)
1 1/2 cups Beef Broth
1/2 cup Plain Whole Milk Yogurt (do not use nonfat or it will curdle)
6 ozs Egg Noodles
1/2 tsp Sea Salt
1/2 tsp Onion Powder
1/2 tsp Black Pepper
1 tbsp Dijon Mustard
3 tbsps Worcestershire Sauce
2 tbsps Corn Starch
1/4 cup Fresh Parsley Or Dill (optional)

NUTRITION

AMOUNT PER SERVING

Calories	320	Fiber	2g
Fat	7g	Sugar	3g
Carbs	31g	Protein	32g

DIRECTIONS

01 Cook egg noodles as directed on packet. Once cooked drain and set to the side.

02 In a small jug, combine beef broth, mustard, onion powder and Worcestershire sauce.

03 Season beef with salt and pepper and place in the slow cooker.

04 Add sliced mushrooms and onion to the slow cooker and pour over beef broth/mustard mix. Cook on low for 5-6 hours or high for 3-4 hours (meat should be very tender).

05 Cut the zucchini in half lengthways and use a vegetable peeler to create long ribbons. Cut into smaller 2-3" lengths. Add to slow cooker along with the yogurt and allow to cook for 10 minutes on high.

06 Carefully scoop out some liquid from the slow cooker (approximately 1/4 cup). In a small bowl mix with corn starch to form a thin paste. Stir mixture back into the slow cooker and allow to cook for an additional 5 minutes or until the sauce thickens.

07 Stir through egg noodles and allow to heat through. Divide between bowl and garnish with fresh parsley or dill.

NOTES

PASTA MEASURE
3 oz of dried egg noodles is approximately 1 cup.

DEEPER FLAVOUR
Sauté mushrooms and onions in a small amount of olive oil with some fresh garlic before adding to slow cooker.

NO CRIMINI
Use white button mushrooms instead.

Dry Rub Pulled Pork

8 SERVINGS 8 HOURS

INGREDIENTS

2-4 lbs Pork Shoulder Roast
1 tbsp Paprika
1 tbsp Brown Sugar
1/2 tsp Black Pepper
1/2 tsp Garlic Powder
1/2 tsp Onion Powder
1/2 tsp Sea Salt
2 tbsps Apple Cider Vinegar
1/2 cup Water

NUTRITION

AMOUNT PER SERVING

Calories	200	Fiber	0g
Fat	11g	Sugar	1g
Carbs	2g	Protein	21g

DIRECTIONS

01 Mix together spices and rub into all sides of the pork.

02 Place vinegar and water in the bottom of the slow cooker.

03 Cover and cook on low for 8 hours or until meat can easily be pulled apart with a fork.

04 Shred pork and remove any of the fatty pieces. Add juices from the slow cooker if the meat needs a little more moisture.

NOTES

HOW TO USE
Use for the pulled pork lettuce cups or simply add to buns with coleslaw for a quick and easy meal. Can be used in the loaded fried rice or to make burrito bowls or tostadas.

STORAGE
Refrigerate for 4-5 days or mix with BBQ sauce and freeze for up to 3 months.

LOW & SLOW FOR THE WIN
Slow cooker pulled pork is best done on the low setting. Be patient and wait the whole 8 hours, it'll be worth it.

TYPE OF PORK
The best cut of meat to make pulled pork comes from the shoulder cut. Depending on your store it may also be sold as Boston butt or picnic roast. When in doubt, ask your butcher.

Pulled Pork Lettuce Cups

4 SERVINGS 20 MINUTES

INGREDIENTS

1 lb Pulled Pork (recipe, page 108)
1/2 cup Bbq Sauce
4 cups Coleslaw Mix
1/2 cup Coleslaw Dressing
1 head Butter Lettuce
2 ears Corn On The Cob

NUTRITION

AMOUNT PER SERVING

Calories	496	Fiber	4g
Fat	24g	Sugar	23g
Carbs	39g	Protein	25g

DIRECTIONS

01 Bring a large pot of water to the boil. Cut the corn in half and cook for 5-7 minutes or until done.

02 Combine pulled pork, BBQ sauce and 1-2 tbsp water. Reheat in a small skillet over low until warmed through. Adjust BBQ sauce portion (more or less) depending on your preference. The water is added to assist in the heating (adjust as needed).

03 Combine coleslaw mix and dressing.

04 Wash the butter lettuce and break apart to create little 'cups'.

05 To serve, place the coleslaw mix, pulled pork and lettuce cups on the table. Place a scoop of the coleslaw into the lettuce cup and top with pulled pork.

06 Serve with cooked corn. Add hot sauce or BBQ sauce for extra flavor.

NOTES

FEEDING KIDS
Before adding the BBQ sauce to the pulled pork, remove a small portion and let kids add their own BBQ sauce or ketchup.

SERVING OPTIONS
Serve pulled pork in lettuce cups, in soft whole grain buns, over rice or coleslaw.

Sausage, Apple & Sauteed Cabbage

4 SERVINGS 30 MINUTES

INGREDIENTS

1 lb Pork Sausage

6 cups Green Cabbage (shredded or finely sliced)

1 Red Onion (Sliced)

1 Green Apple (peeled, cored and sliced into thin wedges)

2 tbsps Soy Sauce Or Tamari (Gf)

2 tsps Extra Virgin Olive Oil

NUTRITION

AMOUNT PER SERVING

Calories	457	Fiber	5g
Fat	35g	Sugar	10g
Carbs	19g	**Protein**	17g

DIRECTIONS

01 Heat oil in a large skillet, cook sausages for 3-4 minutes each side until browned (but not quite cooked). Add onions while the sausages are cooking.

02 Add shredded cabbage and sliced apple to the skillet (moving the sausages to the side), add soy sauce and cook for 10 minutes or until cabbage is soft and sausages are cooked through.

03 Divide between plates. Enjoy.

NOTES

LEFTOVERS
Refrigerate in an airtight container up to 3 days.

OTHER VEGETABELS
Add other vegetables such as mushrooms, Brussel sprouts or bean sprouts to the mix.

ADDITIONAL SIDES
Serve with mashed potato, roasted root vegetables or rice.

Sweet Balsamic Pork Tenderloin

8 SERVINGS 30 MINUTES

INGREDIENTS

2 lbs Pork Tenderloin
1/4 cup Soy Sauce Or Tamari (Gf)
2 tbsps Balsamic Vinegar
2 tbsps Brown Sugar
2 cloves Garlic (crushed)

NUTRITION

AMOUNT PER SERVING

Calories	179	Fiber	0g
Fat	4g	Sugar	3g
Carbs	3g	**Protein**	31g

DIRECTIONS

01 Combine soy sauce, balsamic vinegar, garlic and brown sugar.

02 Place pork tenderloin into a large ziplock bag and pour marinade over top. Place in the fridge for at least an hour. Can be done up to 24 hours ahead.

03 Preheat grill/BBQ to 375F. Place pork tenderloin on the lightly oiled grill. Close lid.

04 Cook for 5 minutes and then turn. Add any leftover marinade. Continue to cook for 5 min per side until each 4 sides are done. Internal temperature should reach 140F-145F.

05 Cover with tin foil and allow to rest for 10 min. Slice and serve.

NOTES

NO GRILL?
Preheat oven to 400F. In a large oven-proof skillet, over medium-heat, add 1 tbsp of oil. Sear (brown) pork tenderloin on all sides, turning with tongs - around 45 seconds/side. Transfer to oven and cook for 18-20 minutes or until internal temperature reaches 145F. Cover with tin foil and allow to rest for 10 minutes.

SERVE WITH
Warm Roasted Vegetables Salad (pg.43).

FREEZER PREP
Marinade pork, place in a freezer safe bag and freeze (uncooked) for up to 3 months.

Snacks & Treats

Apple & Blackberry Cobbler

Chia Pudding

Chocolate Apricot Energy Balls

Chocolate Peanut Butter Energy Balls

Dairy Free Tropical Ice Cream

Grown Up PB & J

Golden Milk

Wonder Bars

Raw Chocolate & Fruit

The Best Movie Popcorn

Apple & Blackberry Cobbler

10 SERVINGS 1 HOUR

INGREDIENTS

2 Green Apple (Granny Smiths, peeled, cored and thinly sliced)
2 cups Blackberries (fresh or frozen)
1 tsp Cinnamon
1/4 cup Orange Juice
2 tbsps Orange Zest (grated)
2 Eggs (room temperature)
2 tbsps Brown Sugar
3/4 cup Granulated Sugar
1/2 cup Butter (melted and slightly cooled)
1/4 cup Sour Cream (2-5% milk fat)
1 tsp Vanilla Extract
1 cup All Purpose Gluten Free Flour (Robin Hood Brand)
1/8 tsp Sea Salt

NUTRITION

AMOUNT PER SERVING

Calories	237	**Fiber**		5g
Fat	10g	**Sugar**		20g
Carbs	36g	**Protein**		2g

DIRECTIONS

01 Preheat oven to 325F.

02 Mix together 1 tbsp. granulated sugar and 1/8 tsp cinnamon, set aside.

03 Place sliced apples, blackberries, brown sugar, orange zest, orange juice and cinnamon, in a large bowl. Gently toss to combine all ingredients. Pour fruit mixture evenly into an 8" x 11" casserole dish.

04 Crack eggs into a large bowl. Using an electric mixer, beat egg on medium speed for 2 minutes or until very fluffy.

05 Keep mixer at medium speed and slowly pour in sugar. Turn mixer to low and pour in melted butter, vanilla extract and sour cream, mix until just combined.

06 Sift the flour and salt, then slowly pour into batter mix. Mix on low until just combined.

07 Pour batter over fruit, covering completely. Sprinkle sugar, cinnamon mixture evenly over the batter. Bake for 55-60 minutes, until a toothpick inserted in the middle of the cake comes out clean and the fruit is bubbling around the edges.

NOTES

SERVING SUGGESTIONS
Serve warm with yogurt or ice-cream.

VARIATIONS
Use any variation of seasonal fruit. Stone fruit in summer, apples and rhubarb in Spring, pear and blueberries in fall, the options are endless.

REGULAR FLOUR
Regular, All Purpose Flour can be used in this recipe if gluten intolerance or allergy is not a concern.

Chia Pudding

2 SERVINGS 10 MINUTES

INGREDIENTS

1/4 cup Chia Seeds
1 cup Unsweetened Oat Milk
1/2 cup Frozen Berries (or other fresh or frozen fruit)
1/2 tsp Cinnamon
1 tsp Vanilla Extract
2 tsps Maple Syrup

NUTRITION

AMOUNT PER SERVING

Calories	225	Fiber	9g
Fat	11g	Sugar	11g
Carbs	28g	**Protein**	6g

DIRECTIONS

01 In a jar or container, combine chia seeds, oat milk, cinnamon, vanilla and maple syrup. Use a fork to mix well, secure lid and vigorously shake for 20-30 second. Stir through berries, refrigerate for at least 2 hours or overnight.

02 Enjoy.

NOTES

STORAGE
Store covered in the fridge for up to 4 to 5 days.

MAKE IT FANCY
Pour half of the chia into a container and let it set for 1-2 hours. Add a layer of pureed fruit (kiwi fruit shown in picture) and top with remaining chia pudding. Top with additional sliced fruit or berries.

NO OAT MILK
Use any other type of milk instead.

WRONG CONSISTANCY?
If the chia pudding is too thin, add 1-2 TBSP additional chia, allow to set for an extra 1-2 hours. If the chia pudding is too thick add a small amount of additional liquid.

Chocolate Apricot Energy Balls

12 SERVINGS 15 MINUTES

INGREDIENTS

1 cup Pitted Dates (packed)
1 cup Walnuts
1/4 cup Hemp Seeds
1/3 cup Cacao Powder
1/2 cup Unsweetened Coconut Flakes (Optional - for coating the energy balls)
1/4 cup Quick Oats
1/4 cup Dried Apricots (diced)

NUTRITION

AMOUNT PER SERVING

Calories	168	Fiber	3g
Fat	11g	Sugar	10g
Carbs	16g	**Protein**	4g

DIRECTIONS

01 Cover dates with warm water and soak for 10-15 minutes. Drain water.

02 Place dates, walnuts, hemp seeds, oats and cocoa powder into the food processor bowl. Process until you get a cookie-dough texture, scraping down the sides as necessary.

03 Stir through dried apricots. Roll the dough into 2-inch balls. Roll energy balls in shredded coconut and place in an airtight container. Makes approximately 24 balls.

04 Refrigerate at least 1 hour to set. Enjoy!

NOTES

SERVING SIZE
Nutrition information is calculated based on 2 balls per serving.

STORAGE
Store in an airtight container in the fridge up to 1 week, or in the freezer for up to 1 month.

NO WALNUTS
Use pecans or almonds instead.

NO HEMPSEEDS
Use chia seed, sesame seeds or pumpkin seeds. Or simply omit and add 1/4 cup more nuts.

ADD WATER
If the mixture is too dry and does not stick together, add 1 tbsp of water to the processor and blend again. Repeat this until you get a 'cookie dough' consistency.

Chocolate Peanut butter Energy Balls

8 SERVINGS 15 MINUTES

INGREDIENTS

1 1/2 cups Pitted Dates
1/4 cup Dried Cranberries
3/4 cup Quick Oats (raw)
3 tbsps Cacao Powder
1/4 cup Peanut Butter
1/8 tsp Sea Salt

NUTRITION

AMOUNT PER SERVING

Calories	179	Fiber	4g
Fat	5g	Sugar	22g
Carbs	33g	**Protein**	4g

DIRECTIONS

01 Add the dates to the bowl of a food processor. Run the processor until the dates are chopped and begin to form a ball.

02 Add the oats, cacao powder, cranberries, sea salt and peanut butter to the dates. Run the food processor until everything is well combined. The mixture should resemble crumbled cookies, but it should stick together when you press it between your fingers.

03 Form the mixture into small, 1" balls with your hands. Place in the refrigerator for at least 10 minutes to set. Mixture makes approximately 24 balls. A serving is 3 balls.

04 Keep in the fridge for up to a week, or in the freezer for up to 3 months.

NOTES
NO PEANUT BUTTER
Use almond or cashew butter instead.

SERVING SIZE
One serving is equal to three balls.

STORAGE
Store in the fridge for up to five days, or in the freezer for up to three months.

DRY MIXTURE
If the mixture is too dry to form into balls, place the ingredients back into the food process. Run the food processor and 1tbsp of water at a time until your mixture comes together.

STICKY MIXTURE
If the mixture is too sticky, add 1-2 tbsp of extra oats until you get the right consistency.

MAKE THEM SALTY
Roll in crushed, salted peanuts.

Dairy Free Tropical Ice Cream

2 SERVINGS 5 MINUTES

INGREDIENTS

2 Banana (sliced and frozen)
1/2 cup Frozen Mango
2 tbsps Canned Coconut Milk
1/2 Lime (juice)

NUTRITION

AMOUNT PER SERVING

Calories	159	Fiber	4g
Fat	3g	Sugar	20g
Carbs	34g	**Protein**	2g

DIRECTIONS

01 Add frozen bananas, mango, lime juice and coconut milk to food processor and blend. Occasionally scrape down the sides and continue to blend until smooth (approximately 3 to 5 minutes).

02 Scoop into a bowl and enjoy immediately as soft serve or for firmer ice cream, place in an airtight, freezer-safe container and freeze for at least 1 hour before scooping.

NOTES

FRESH HERBS
Add 1-2 tbsps of fresh cilantro or mint.

MORE SCOOPABLE
Add 1 tbsp vodka to prevent hard freeze.

LEFTOVERS
Freeze in an airtight container for up to three months.

SALTED CHOCOLATE, PEANUT BUTTER, PECAN
Skip the mango and coconut milk and add 2 tbsp. peanut butter, 1/4 cup chopped pecans, 2 tbsp. dark chocolate (chopped) and a pinch of sea salt. Blend as per instructions.

Grown Up PB & J

1 SERVING 5 MINUTES

INGREDIENTS

1 Plain Rice Cake
1 tbsp Peanut Butter
2 tbsps Frozen Berries (thawed - or use fresh)
1 tbsp Hemp Seeds

NUTRITION

AMOUNT PER SERVING

Calories	196	Fiber	2g
Fat	13g	Sugar	4g
Carbs	14g	**Protein**	8g

DIRECTIONS

01 Spread rice cake with peanut butter. Place berries on top and sprinkle with hemp seeds.

NOTES

DIFFERENT SEEDS
Use chia seeds or a mixture of the two.

NO PEANUT BUTTER
Use almond butter, sunflower butter or swap for cream cheese.

Golden Milk

2 SERVINGS 10 MINUTES

INGREDIENTS

2 cups Plain Coconut Milk (Try SoDelicious or Silk coconut milk)
1/2 tsp Ground Ginger (or 1 tsp fresh)
1/2 tsp Turmeric (ground/dry)
1/2 tsp Cinnamon
2 tsp Honey
1 Pinch Pepper

NUTRITION

AMOUNT PER SERVING

Calories	114	Fiber	1g
Fat	5g	Sugar	15g
Carbs	17g	**Protein**	0g

DIRECTIONS

01 Combine all ingredients into a small saucepan. Whisk all ingredients together and gently heat for 3-5 minutes - do not boil.

02 Divide between two mugs. Enjoy

NOTES

USE FRESH TURMERIC AND GINGER ROOT
Skip the turmeric and ginger powder and use fresh instead. Grate each root and use 1/2 tsp per serving. Increase the amount if you like it a little more 'spicy'

AVOID A MESS
Rinse all glasses and mugs out right after use to avoid turmeric stains. Use baking soda on turmeric stains if they do happen.

VEGAN
Use maple syrup to sweeten instead of honey.

WHY PEPPER?
The chemical piperine (found in pepper) enhances the absorption of curcumin (found in turmeric) boosting it's anti-inflammatory properties.

ADD COCONUT OIL OR GHEE
If using almond, cashew or other low fat milks, add 1 tsp of coconut oil or ghee. Fat enhances the absorption of the spices.

Wonder Bars

16 SERVINGS 15 MINUTES

INGREDIENTS

- **1 cup** Rolled Oats
- **1/2 cup** Brown Rice Crispies
- **1/4 cup** Dried Cranberries
- **1/2 cup** Almonds (chopped)
- **1/4 cup** Hemp Seeds
- **1/4 cup** Vanilla Protein Powder
- **1/3 cup** All Natural Peanut Butter
- **1/4 cup** Raw Honey
- **2 tbsps** Coconut Oil
- **1/4 cup** Dark Chocolate Chips

DIRECTIONS

01. Combine all dry ingredients in a large bowl.
02. Place honey, peanut butter and coconut oil in a small pan over low heat. Continuously stir until melted and smooth.
03. Pour peanut butter mixture over dry mix. Use a large spoon and mix well until everything is coated evenly.
04. Pour mixture into a cake tin lined with cling wrap. Fold the cling wrap over the top of the mixture and press down firmly with you hands so that everything 'sticks' together.
05. Place in the freezer to 'set' for at least 30 minutes or leave in the fridge overnight. Cut into 16 pieces and store in the fridge for up to 2 weeks.

NUTRITION

AMOUNT PER SERVING

Calories	161	Fiber	2g
Fat	10g	Sugar	8g
Carbs	15g	**Protein**	5g

NOTES

VARIATIONS

Use any combination of dried fruit, nuts or seeds that you like.

Raw Chocolate

4 SERVINGS 10 MINUTES

INGREDIENTS

- **2 tbsps** Cocoa Powder
- **2 tbsps** Cacao Butter (melted)
- **1 tbsp** Maple Syrup

NUTRITION

AMOUNT PER SERVING

Calories	79	Fiber	1g
Fat	7g	Sugar	3g
Carbs	5g	Protein	1g

DIRECTIONS

01 Make a double boiler by placing a small saucepan into a large saucepan that has been filled with 1/3 water.

02 Grate cocoa butter and add to the small saucepan, heat until melted.

03 In a small bowl combine cocoa powder, melted cocoa butter and maple syrup. Stir until well combined and the mixture resembles chocolate sauce.

04 Use as directed in notes. Place in the fridge to set for 10-15 minutes.

NOTES

CHOCOLATE COVERED FRUIT
Drizzle melted chocolate over fruit (such as strawberries). Place in the fridge to set.

FRUIT & NUT CHOCOLATE
Combine 1 cup of mixed nuts, seeds and dried fruit. Pour melted chocolate over the mixture and combine will. Pour out onto a baking tray (or plate) line with baking paper. Flatten down to around 1/2" thick. Allow to set in the fridge.

MAKE IT SPICY
Add a pinch or cayenne pepper to the chocolate mix.

SALTY
Sprinkle a pinch of sea salt or pink Himalayan rock salt over the chocolate before it sets.

FLAVOUR
Add a 1/4 tsp peppermint or orange extract to the chocolate mix.

The Best Movie Popcorn

2 SERVINGS 5 MINUTES

INGREDIENTS

1/4 cup Popcorn Kernels
2 tbsps Nutritional Yeast
2 tbsps Butter

NUTRITION

AMOUNT PER SERVING

Calories	222	Fiber	5g
Fat	13g	Sugar	0g
Carbs	20g	**Protein**	8g

DIRECTIONS

01 Pop the corn kernels in an air popper.

02 Melt butter and drizzle over popcorn. Sprinkle over nutritional yeast, mix well to distribute the yeast and butter. Enjoy.

NOTES

NO BUTTER
Use melted coconut oil instead.

Index

A

Apple & Blackberry Cobbler, 114
Apple & Cinnamon Oatmeal, 14
Avocado French Toast with Egg, 20

B

BACON

    Broccoli & Bacon Pasta Salad with BBQ Chicken, 39
    Creamy Pea Pesto & Bacon Pasta, 86

BEEF

    Camping Chili, 102
    Classic Shepherd's Pie, 103
    Grilled Lemon Garlic Steak Skewers, 104
    Montreal Steak Salad, 42
    Muffin Tin Mini Meatloaf, 105
    Satay Beef Skewers, 106
    Skinny Beef Stroganoff, 107
    Soy & Ginger Beef Stir Fry, 97
    Weeknight Spaghetti Bolognese, 93

Bocconcini Tomato Pesto Lunch Bowl, 28

BREAKFAST

    Apple & Cinnamon Oatmeal, 14
    Avocado French Toast with Egg, 20
    Breakfast Burritos, 21
    Breakfast Smoothie, 19
    Egg Muffins, 22
    Eggs with Sweet Potato Toast, 23
    Fried Egg Breakfast Salad, 24
    Granola, 16
    Muesli, 17
    Overnight Oats, 15
    Vanilla Banana Chia Pudding, 25
    Warm Barley Breakfast, 18

Broccoli & Bacon Pasta Salad with BBQ Chicken, 39
Buddha Bowl with Crispy Tofu, 53
Buffalo Chicken Bites, 66
Buffalo Chicken Salad, 38
Butternut Squash Soup, 46

C

Camping Chili, 102
Chia Pudding, 25, 115

CHICKEN

    Broccoli & Bacon Pasta Salad with BBQ Chicken, 39
    Buffalo Chicken Bites, 66
    Buffalo Chicken Salad, 38
    Chicken Enchiladas, 67
    Chicken Pot Pie, 69
    Chicken Satay Stir Fry, 95
    Cilantro Lime Chicken, 70
    Creamy Sundried Tomato & Mushroom Pasta, 89
    Creamy Tomato Chicken with Green Vegetables, 88
    Deconstructed Chicken Parmigiana, 71
    Fresh Summer Rolls with Spicy Peanut Sauce, 72
    Mango Salsa Chicken Cups, 76
    Mulligatawny Soup, 49
    Pesto Gnocchi Skillet with Broccoli & Sausage, 91
    Prosciutto Wrapped Stuffed Chicken Breast, 78
    Quick & Easy Chicken Tostadas, 77
    Sheet Pan Chicken Fajitas, 79
    Sheet Pan Pesto Chicken & Grilled Vegetables, 83
    Skillet Chicken Bruschetta Pasta, 90
    Slow Cooker Thai Chicken Noodle Soup, 51

Cilantro Lime Chicken, 70

D

Dairy Free Tropical Ice Cream, 118
Deconstructed Chicken Parmigiana, 71
Dry Rub Pulled Pork, 108

E

EGGS

    Avocado French Toast with Egg, 20
    Breakfast Burritos, 21
    Egg Muffins, 22
    Eggs with Sweet Potato Toast, 23
    Fried Egg Breakfast Salad, 24

F
Falafel Bowl, 55
Flaked Salmon with Beans & Arugula Salad, 35
Fresh Summer Rolls with Spicy Peanut Sauce, 72
Fried Egg Breakfast Salad, 24

G
Garden Salad, 29
Garlic Shrimp & Baby Spinach Pasta, 87
Goat's Cheese, Prosciutto, Pear & Walnut Salad, 41
Golden Milk, 120
Granola, 16
Grilled Lemon Garlic Steak Skewers, 104
Grilled Salmon & Peach Salad, 36
Grilled Turkey Koftas, 74
Grown Up PB & J, 119

H
Honey Garlic Shrimp Stir Fry, 96

I
Italian Turkey Stuffed Peppers, 75

J
Jessi's Favorite Toasties, 52

L
Lentil Patties, 62
Lentil, Artichoke & Sundried Tomato Salad, 31
Loaded Fried Rice, 57

M
Mango Salsa Chicken Cups, 78
Minestrone Soup with Meatballs, 50
Montreal Steak Salad, 42
Muesli, 17
Muffin Tin Mini Meatloaf, 105
Mulligatawny Soup, 49

O
OATS
    Apple & Cinnamon Oatmeal, 14
    Granola, 16
    Muesli, 17
    Overnight Oats, 15
    Chocolate Apricot Energy Balls, 116
    Chocolate Peanut Butter Energy Balls, 117
    Wonder Bars, 121

Overnight Oats, 15

PASTA
    Broccoli & Bacon Pasta Salad with BBQ Chicken, 39
    Creamy Pea Pesto & Bacon Pasta, 86
    Creamy Sundried Tomato & Mushroom Pasta, 89
    Creamy Tomato Chicken with Green Vegetables, 88
    Garlic Shrimp & Baby Spinach Pasta, 87
    Minestrone Soup with Meatballs
    Pesto Gnocchi Skillet with Broccoli & Sausage, 91
    Skillet Chicken Bruschetta Pasta, 90
    Skinny Beef Stroganoff, 107
    Weeknight Spaghetti Bolognese, 93

PLANT BASED
    Buddha Bowl with Crispy Tofu, 53
    Falafel Bowl, 55
    Lentil Patties, 62
    Loaded Fried Rice, 57
    Red Lentil Shepherd's Pie, 59
    Zucchini & Corn Fritters, 63

Prosciutto Wrapped Stuffed Chicken Breast, 80
Pulled Pork Lettuce Cups, 109

PORK
    Dry Rub Pulled Pork, 108
    Pulled Pork Lettuce Cups, 109
    Sausage, Apple & Sautéed Cabbage, 110
    Sweet Balsamic Pork Tenderloin, 111

Q
Quick & Easy Chicken Tostadas, 79
Quinoa Salad, 32

R
Raw Chocolate & Fruit, 122
Red Lentil Shepherd's Pie, 59

S
SALALD
    Bocconcini, Tomato, Pesto Lunch Bowl, 28
    Broccoli & Bacon Pasta Salad with BBQ Chicken, 39

SALAD CONTINUED
    Buffalo Chicken Salad, 38
    Flaked Salmon with Beans & Arugula Salad, 35
    Garden Salad, 29
    Goat's Cheese, Prosciutto, Pear & Walnut Salad, 41
    Grilled Salmon & Peach Salad, 36
    Lentil, Artichoke & Sundried Tomato Salad, 31
    Montreal Steak Salad, 42
    Quinoa Salad, 32
    Strawberry, Asparagus & Goats Cheese Salad, 33
    Tuna Stack with Fresh Tomato Salsa, 37
    Warm Roast Vegetable Salad, 43

Salmon & Sweet Potato Cakes, 61
Satay Beef Skewers, 106
Sausage, Apple & Sautéed Cabbage, 110

SEAFOOD
    Flaked Salmon with Beans & Arugula Salad, 35
    Garlic Shrimp & Baby Spinach Pasta, 87
    Grilled Salmon & Peach Salad, 36
    Honey Garlic Shrimp Stir Fry
    Salmon & Sweet Potato Cakes, 61
    Tuna Stack with Fresh Tomato Salsa, 37

Sheet Pan Chicken Fajitas, 79
Sheet Pan Mini Meat Loaf with Vegetables, 82
Sheet Pan Pesto Chicken & Grilled Vegetables, 83
Skillet Chicken Bruschetta Pasta, 90
Skinny Beef Stroganoff, 107
Slow Cooker Thai Chicken Noodle Soup, 51

SNACKS
    Chocolate Apricot Energy Balls, 116
    Chocolate Peanut Butter Energy Balls, 117
    Grown Up PB & J, 119
    The Best Movie Popcorn, 123
    Wonder Bars, 121

SOUP
    Butternut Squash Soup, 46
    Creamy Potato & Ham Soup, 47
    Minestrone Soup with Meatballs, 50
    Mulligatawny Soup, 49
    Slow Cooker Thai Chicken Noodle Soup, 51

    Soy & Ginger Beef Stir Fry, 97
    Spicy Peanuts Sauce, 73

STIR FRY
    Honey Garlic Shrimp Stir Fry, 96
    Soy & Ginger Beef Stir Fry, 97
    Teriyaki Meatballs & Stir Fry Vegetables, 98
    Chicken Satay Stir Fry, 95

Strawberry, Asparagus & Goats Cheese Salad, 33
Sweet Balsamic Pork Tenderloin, 111

T
Taco Seasoning, 81
Teriyaki Meatballs & Stir Fry Vegetables, 98
The Best Movie Popcorn, 123

TREATS
    Dairy Free Tropical Ice Cream, 118
    Raw Chocolate & Fruit, 122

Tuna Stack with Fresh Tomato Salsa, 37

TURKEY
    Grilled Turkey Koftas, 76
    Italian Turkey Stuffed Peppers, 75
    Sheet Pan Mini Meat Loaf with Vegetables, 82
    Teriyaki Meatballs & Stir Fry Vegetables, 98

V
Vanilla Banana Chia Pudding, 25

W
Warm Barley Breakfast, 18
Warm Roast Vegetable Salad, 43
Weeknight Spaghetti Bolognese, 93
Wonder Bars, 121

Z
Zucchini & Corn Fritters, 63

Thank you again for choosing The Balanced Four Cookbook. The beauty of cooking, making your own meals and living a healthy life, is it's an ever evolving practice. I'm always experimenting in the kitchen, making new creations and sharing new videos through my social media platforms. Come and connect with me online for more delicious recipes and simple ways to live a more balanced life.

Use the QR code below to find me online, watch my latest cooking video, book a nutrition coaching package or find out more about The Balanced Four Membership. And as a special thank you, enjoy 50% off your first month by using the code: cookbookvip

The Balanced Four Membership is like having a nutrition coach, a meal planning expert and a cheer squad on call! Ready to help you simplify the meal time hustle and live your healthiest, best life.

In health & happiness,

Jessi

Notes

Notes

Notes

Notes

Made in the USA
Columbia, SC
28 May 2021